CW00794727

END OF THE ROAD

FINANCIAL TIMES
Prentice Hall

In an increasingly competitive world, it is quality
of thinking that gives an edge – an idea that opens new
doors, a technique that solves a problem, or an insight
that simply helps make sense of it all.

We work with leading authors in the fields of
management and finance to bring cutting-edge thinking
and best learning practice to a global market.

Under a range of leading imprints, including
Financial Times Prentice Hall, we create world-class
print publications and electronic products giving
readers knowledge and understanding which can then
be applied, whether studying or at work.

To find out more about our business and professional
products, you can visit us at www.business-minds.com

For other Pearson Education publications, visit
www.pearsoned-ema.com

Pearson
Education

END OF THE ROAD

BMW and ROVER

A BRAND TOO FAR

CHRIS BRADY &
ANDREW LORENZ

FINANCIAL TIMES
Prentice Hall

an imprint of Pearson Education
London • New York • San Francisco • Toronto • Sydney • Tokyo • Singapore • Hong Kong
Cape Town • Madrid • Paris • Milan • Munich • Amsterdam

PEARSON EDUCATION LIMITED

Head Office:
Edinburgh Gate
Harlow CM20 2JE
Tel: +44 (0)1279 623623
Fax: +44 (0)1279 431059

London Office:
128 Long Acre
London WC2E 9AN
Tel: +44 (0)20 7447 2000
Fax: +44 (0)20 7240 5771
Website: www.business-minds.com

First published in Great Britain in 2001

© Pearson Education Limited 2001

The right of Chris Brady and Andrew Lorenz to be identified as authors
of this work has been asserted by them in accordance
with the Copyright, Designs and Patents Act 1988.

ISBN 0 273 65300 8

British Library Cataloguing in Publication Data
A CIP catalogue record for this book can be obtained from the British Library.

10 9 8 7 6 5 4 3 2 1

Designed by George Hammond Design, Diss, Norfolk
Typeset by Northern Phototypesetting Co. Ltd, Bolton
Printed and bound in Great Britain by Redwood Books, Trowbridge

The Publishers' policy is to use paper manufactured from sustainable forests.

Contents

To Helen Lorenz and Jim Brady for what they mean to us

About the authors

Andrew Lorenz, former Business Editor of *The Sunday Times*, is currently a Director of Financial Dynamics Business Communications. His previous roles have included Deputy City Editor of the *Sunday Telegraph*, City correspondent on *The Scotsman* as well as Industrial Editor at *The Journal*, Newcastle.

He broke the story that Rover was going to be sold, three months before it was announced, and he is acknowledged as the authority on the subject.

Andrew has published many articles and columns which have featured in *Management Today*, *Auto Express*, *Defence Procurement*, *Stock Exchange* magazine, *Acquisitions Monthly*, *TGWU Journal*, and has had contributions broadcast on BBC radio and ITV television.

Dr Chris Brady is currently the Director of Studies for the General and Strategic Management MBA at the City University Business School, London and Head Business Coach at Cape Consulting. He previously served in an intelligence capacity as a Royal Navy officer during the Falkland and Gulf conflicts and more recently in the Balkans. He has also worked in the gambling and construction industries, as well as working for Chrysler in Detroit during his teens. Dr Brady is a qualified UEFA A licence football coach. He played and coached football to semi-professional level, which he considers to have been his greatest managerial challenge.

He has published on topics as varied as US foreign policy, Cabinet government, teamwork, education, the environment, intelligence failures and the United Nations.

Chris Brady is also a visiting lecturer and adviser on decision-making issues at the Joint Services Command and Staff College, the military's senior staff college. He lectures to the senior staff of the Kuwaiti Staff College and is a Research Fellow of the Institute of Contemporary British History.

Chris interviewed virtually all the major players in the BMW and Rover camps.

Acknowledgements

We would like to thank Rebecca Chambers and Michelle Potter for their support and all the interviewees who gave so generously of their time and memory banks.

Introduction

O N 1 OCTOBER 2000 John Towers, the Chairman of MG Rover Group, explained the current ownership of Rover as a stewardship. 'We are, you could say, looking to get this business into shape and possibly preparing the way for someone else to come in and help look after the long-term future.' An editorial piece in *Marketing Week* (23 March 2000), immediately after the announcement that Alchemy would buy Rover, stated that the 'failure of the 75 epitomised BMW's problems as Rover's "brand steward"'. It seems that everyone wants to 'steward' Rover but nobody wants to 'own' it. 'Owning' appears to entail far too much responsibility, accountability and risk. This book tells the story of one attempt to genuinely 'own' Rover and to return it to its former glories.

When the two authors sat down to write this fascinating story we were drawn by the usual characteristics. The journalist was drawn by the story itself, by the intrigue, the personalities, the colour. The academic was drawn by the analytical possibilities, the classical merger and acquisition (M&A) case history, the process. Both of us were surprised at how interesting were the insights the other brought to the table. There was another interesting synergy to be derived from our partnership. As we discussed our respective views as to what had happened with BMW's ownership, it became clear that our assessments of the strength of the Rover brand, at the point of purchase, differed considerably. Delving further it turned out that one of us was the son of a director of a medium-sized company who had been the proud owner of a Rover P5 and one of us was the son of a council worker who had never even owned a car, let alone a Rover.

The point of this information is to explain our relative attachment to the brand. In one it was strong, in the other weak. Both were emotionally driven. It should have come as no surprise, therefore, subsequently to find that the emotional aspects of this supposedly rational business situation should so dominate the story.

PART ONE

Before BMW

CHAPTER 1

A Coup for Whom?

ARLY ON FRIDAY, 27 JANUARY 1994, a plane carrying George Simpson, Rover's chairman, touched down at Tokyo's Narita airport. After checking into his hotel and freshening up, Simpson had a bite to eat and then headed for a 2 pm meeting with Nobuhiko Kawamoto, president of Honda. As his car made its way to Honda's headquarters, through the sleet of an unusually bitter winter day, Simpson braced himself for a potentially tense and uncomfortable meeting. Eventually he arrived at the Honda building in the central Aoyama district, overlooking the Imperial Palace. As he strode across the foyer, a full range of Honda cars was on display, a range with which Simpson had become intimately involved during Rover's alliance with the Japanese car giant. He did not give them a second glance, however, because his mind was on other more momentous issues.

Simpson rode the elevator to the top floor and was taken to the room where he had frequently met Kawamoto during the long association between Rover and Honda. But Kawamoto did not appear. Instead, Simpson was met by Honda's finance director along with Kawamoto's personal adviser. Kawamoto, they said, was unavailable. He obviously had more than an inkling of the purpose of Simpson's visit, hence the failure to appear. Simpson was convinced that his Honda counterpart was determined not to lose face by being the direct recipient of the unpalatable news which the Rover chief was about to deliver. So he simply told Kawamoto's deputies. Two days earlier, he explained, Dr Hagen Luderitz, the director of corporate planning at BMW, had personally offered British Aerospace (BAe) £800m for the entire Rover group. The terms, Simpson told the Honda duo, were superior to Honda's own offer to increase its existing 20 per cent stake in Rover to 47.5 per cent. He was right, because while Honda held out the possibility of a stock market flotation of Rover several years down the track, there was no guarantee that this would ever happen. By contrast, BMW's bid gave BAe, which had bought Rover in 1988, a clean exit from the vehicles business – and a total and immediate exit was the top priority for the financially stretched aerospace group.

Simpson said later, 'I tried to explain that I was very sorry, that Western business had to deal with issues such as shareholder value, that it was extremely difficult to evaluate things like a 15-year partnership and moral commitments, but that when the sums were done the bird in the hand, the £800m, was worth more than Honda had offered.' Simpson asked whether Honda wanted to reconsider its refusal to buy the whole of Rover. The answer was no. Rover, the Honda executives said, had to remain a British company or it would lose its identity. After three painful hours, the meeting was over. Simpson returned to his hotel for the night and on Saturday morning, 24 hours after arriving in Tokyo, he was on his way home. That night, in a private room of a Bavarian restaurant, the papers were signed. Britain's last big motor manufacturer was sold to BMW.

> **Simpson asked whether Honda wanted to reconsider its refusal to buy the whole of Rover. The answer was no**

The deal struck between Simpson and BMW was the culmination of BAe's efforts to recover from a near-fatal financial crisis in the early 1990s. BAe's top management team – John Cahill, chairman, Dick Evans, chief executive, and Richard Lapthorne, finance director – were rebuilding the group's balance sheet which had been stricken by the impact of the recession on the conglomerate strategy pursued by Cahill's predecessor, Professor Sir Roland Smith. Smith was ousted by the board in late 1991 and his finance director, Dudley Eustace, left early in 1992. But the mess the company was in took much longer to clear up.

The nadir came on 23 September 1992, when Cahill announced a £129m half-year loss, caused by astronomical losses in BAe's regional aircraft operations. The shares, which had started that day at the lowly figure of 199p (having reached a peak of 733p in 1989, just before the roof fell in), nose-dived to touch 98p at one stage of the traumatic day. Humiliatingly, BAe had to postpone payment of its dividend – the ultimate sin as far as investors were concerned. So bad did the situation look that some City analysts thought the company was going bankrupt.

Behind the scenes, Cahill, Evans and Lapthorne – despite personal tensions that resulted in the chairman leaving after Rover had been sold – had decided BAe's only hope of salvation lay in the retention of its defence operations plus Airbus, and the sale of everything else. Rover was by far the largest element in the non-core businesses. By reversing Smith's conglomerization and stripping away underperforming activities, the BAe team could ensure that the large profits of the defence side would flow through undiluted to the group's bottom line, reviving the shares.

The decision to sell Rover was a tightly held secret. To the outside world, BAe maintained the position that: Rover is a core business. It had to. If word had leaked out that Rover was on the block, dealers and customers would have melted away and there would have been no worthwhile business left to sell. Inside the car industry, however, BAe's lack of long-term commitment to Rover was obvious. To a certain extent that explained the timing of BMW's initial interest in Rover. In June 1993 Bernd Pischetsrieder coincidentally met George Simpson at a meeting of the presidents' club for European car-company chiefs. Pischetsrieder, 45, had recently sprung to prominence as the surprise choice to succeed the aristocratic Eberhard von Kuenheim, who had headed BMW for 23 years as chairman of the management board. Outside BMW, Pischetsrieder was a complete unknown – most people could not even pronounce his name, let alone spell it (it actually means 'he who gathers wood for the bishop'). BMW watchers had always expected von Kuenheim to be succeeded by Wolfgang Reitzle, the group's engineering chief, who was widely regarded as something of a genius in product design and development.

However, in the early 1990s, Reitzle had blotted his copybook, in the eyes of von Kuenheim and Johanna Quandt, the matriarch whose family effectively controlled BMW through a 46 per cent shareholding, by flirting with a move to Porsche. Loyalty is highly prized by the Quandts and, although Reitzle opted to stay in Munich, his dalliance with Porsche had fatally damaged his leadership ambitions. So, while von Kuenheim, the trusted lieutenant of Johanna and her late husband Herbert Quandt, became chairman of BMW's supervisory board, Pischetsrieder emerged as the dark horse to take what is, under the German dual board structure, effectively the post of chief executive.

Pischetsrieder, a Bavarian former operations engineer and chief technical planner was, ironically, also the great-nephew of Sir Alec Issigonis, designer of the Mini. As the new chief executive he took on von Kuenheim's mantle at a time when the Munich carmaker, like its archrival Mercedes-Benz, was at a crossroads. For the first time they were facing competition from the Americans and Japanese in the quality car market as well as competition from Rover itself. BMW had reached the same conclusion as Mercedes: it had to increase its own volumes and cut its costs. 'In 10 years it might be that BMW by itself would be too small to compete in the world industry,' Pischetsrieder reflected at the time.

What that meant, to Pischetsrieder at least, was that BMW would have to widen its product base to become a 'full-range' manufacturer, building small cars and four-wheel-drive vehicles as well as its traditional models. Unlike Helmut Werner of Mercedes, however, who decided to attach the Swabian star to his small cars, Pischetsrieder and his strategy director, Luderitz, believed BMW would dilute its image if it went into small cars. What was needed, they concluded, was an additional brand to expand the portfolio.

Pischetsrieder's opening gambit at the meeting with Simpson was to ask whether BAe and Rover would be willing to sell Land Rover, the Solihull based four-wheel-drive business in which von Kuenheim and Reitzle had already shown interest. Land Rover, maker of the Defender, Discovery and Range Rover, was the jewel in Rover's crown because, unlike the loss making cars side, it actually made money. Profits had peaked at £120m in 1990, the first full year of Discovery, and were still running at around £100m a year. In fact, so successful was Land Rover that, by the time Pischetsrieder met with Simpson, BAe itself had considered spinning it off in a stock-market flotation. The drawback to that plan was that it would have left BAe with an unsaleable product – Rover cars without its crown jewel. For BAe, that was no deal.

Simpson told Pischetsrieder that Rover was an integrated business and Land Rover alone was not for sale. The reply suited Pischetsrieder down to the ground. The BMW boss returned to Munich, consulted his closest colleagues, and informed Simpson that he might after all be interested in the whole package. Such a response was music to Simpson's ears. He knew that BAe planned to sell Rover, and after almost 25 years with the company he was concerned that Rover should find a buyer that would simultaneously satisfy BAe's need to maximize proceeds to shareholders and offer the most secure future for Rover's 33,000 workers. Simpson's assessment was that there were only three realistic options: a full takeover by Honda, a management buyout, or acquisition by a German car company. Neither Ford nor General Motors, which in 1985–6 had tried to buy Rover cars and Land Rover, were seen as viable options. The first possibility looked unlikely. As he correctly surmised, Honda had little interest in a bid since its existing relationship, including a 20 per cent stake in Rover cars, delivered all the cost benefits the Japanese needed. The second option, a buyout, was a serious contender. At about the time when Simpson and Pischetsrieder had their first conversation, Simpson and Sir Graham Day, Rover's former chairman, were taking soundings in the City about the feasibility of a buyout. But they quickly ran into trouble in the shape of problems raising finance to support Rover's ongoing investment and working capital needs. Simpson summarized the difficulties:

> " Buyouts are not about getting people to invest in the equity; they are about getting people to organize finance to run the company. Rover needed about £1bn in daily banking capital just to keep going. It was easy to find people to pay £400m or £500m for the equity, but we couldn't find someone to stand behind the £1billion. "

Bruce Pattullo, then chairman of Bank of Scotland, told Simpson: 'My heart says that, for the sake of UK plc, I would love to back this deal. But my head tells me it is unbankable and that is the view my shareholders would take.' That left only the German option.

Volkswagen, which had wanted to buy Rover before it was sold to BAe, was now struggling to come to terms with its breakneck expansion in the late 1980s, but Mercedes and BMW were ideal candidates because they planned to move into the market segments already occupied by Rover. They would, therefore, be likely to look more favourably than Honda at retaining the Rover cars operations at Longbridge in Birmingham and Cowley in Oxford. Because of Werner's go-it-alone strategy, Mercedes showed no interest and left Pischetsrieder a clear run. That suited the handful of Rover executives who knew of the planned sale. They had conducted brainstorming sessions with Professor Kumar Bhattacharyya, head of the Warwick Manufacturing Group based at Warwick University, and had concluded that BMW would be their ideal partner.

August saw the expiry of the five-year deadline within which BAe was effectively barred by the government from selling Rover. Dick Evans, chief executive of BAe, identifies that month as the critical moment leading up to the sale. The following month, another meeting with Pischetsrieder confirmed BMW's interest at a price of £550m, which did not meet BAe's valuation since at that time Rover had a book value of almost £1.3bn. There was clearly scope for negotiation. However, Honda remained a large stumbling block. Pischetsrieder wrote to Kawamoto, asking the Japanese to co-operate in facilitating a Rover–BMW deal that could eventually lead to a BMW–Honda association. Kawamoto didn't even reply.

In November, Simpson and Evans flew to Tokyo to meet Kawamoto and his colleagues. Although negotiations were continuing, with both sides having investment banks on board – Dresdner Kleinwort Benson for BAe and Schroders for Honda – the talks had made little progress. The BAe duo pressed Honda to make an offer for Rover and – to prove that the Japanese were not the only game in town – showed Kawamoto the first offer from BMW. That, at least, provoked a response – albeit not the one BAe had sought. Rather than make a full bid, Honda said it was prepared to raise its 20 per cent Rover stake to 47.5 per cent, with BAe holding 47.5 per cent and the 5 per cent balance going to Rover managers and employees. BAe would hold the stake for up to five years, and then Honda would aim to float Rover on the stock market. Honda also wanted to appoint two directors to the Rover board and, much more contentiously, a number of 'advisers' to shadow the Rover executives. Evans and Simpson were unimpressed: Honda was effectively demanding management control without committing to buy the company. It would neither guarantee BAe a clean exit, nor give BAe a guaranteed exit price for the British group's residual 47.5 per cent stake.

BAe did not like it but, with BMW holding back, Honda's seemed to be the only offer on the table. The Bavarians had been further discouraged when John Towers, Rover's managing director, told BMW that Rover wanted to stay with Honda. Given the cold shoulder by Honda and Towers, Pischetsrieder concluded that BMW could go no further, at least for the moment.

During the rest of November and on through December, the joint Honda–BAe/Rover study team, headed on the British side by Simpson and Lapthorne, continued to work through the permutations of a possible agreement. For BAe the search for a solution gained urgency once Simpson was headhunted to become chief executive of Lucas Industries, a post he would take up by May. Simpson shuttled between London and Tokyo. Early in January, the Honda team flew to London. Everybody knew that time was running out.

Early in January, the Honda team flew to London. Everybody knew that time was running out

Honda, however, refused to budge from its revised offer to raise its holding to 47.5 per cent. It said it would pay about £167m for the additional shares, valuing Rover at about £650m. It pledged to take the business public by 1998, provided Rover met various profit and cash-generation targets. 'Our philosophy was to maintain Rover as an independent British company,' said Shojiro Miyake, president of Honda Motor Europe. In his mind a deal along those lines had been agreed by 21 January.

Simpson and Lapthorne did not see things that way. They had agreed to *consider* the offer, but they did not like it much. Even if flotation occurred in the time-frame suggested by Honda, and that was by no means certain, it still left BAe 'as financier of 50 per cent of Rover's quite large appetite for cash with no management input to control that', according to Lapthorne. More significantly, it also meant that BAe had no guaranteed exit from Rover. Simpson was unconvinced that the performance targets could be met. For that to happen, said Simpson, 'every egg would have to be a bird'. Simpson and Lapthorne asked Honda to give BAe a put option – the right to sell its outstanding shares to Honda, to be exercised if flotation did not take place within the prescribed timetable. Honda refused, believing it was still in the driving seat.

In many respects, Honda's attitude was understandable and reflected its approach to the whole Rover relationship. The Japanese link had, after all, saved Rover from extinction by providing product and manufacturing know-how that Rover would otherwise have fatally lacked, and Honda had increasingly called the tune. Rover paid Honda substantial sums for the car floor-pans and the engines for its larger models, plus a royalty on each jointly developed car Rover sold. Moreover, the companies' technology agreement barred Rover from selling Honda-based models in markets Honda wanted for itself. For example, Rover was not allowed to sell the 600 in America, a market that may well have embraced it. Honda even had a veto over the interior design and styling of the 600, apparently to ensure that it could not outshine Honda's sister model, the Accord.

In order to save itself Rover had mortgaged any future revival and was caught in a Honda bear-hug. The Japanese giant may have given the British company protection, but it also prevented any possibility that the cars side of the business would ever be able to break into real, and maintainable, profit. All Rover could do, and Simpson did it very well, was to squeeze every penny out of the pipeline that Rover itself controlled. By early January, Honda had apparently deposited BAe between a rock and a hard place. BAe was left with the unpalatable choice of bowing to the Japanese terms or rejecting them in the hope a better deal would materialize. Dick Evans said, 'We were involved in some kind of Japanese poker game'. If it was a poker game, then it was stud poker, and Evans's 'hole' card turned out to be an ace.

The game began to reach its crescendo in mid-January, when Evans and Simpson again flew out to see Kawamoto. Evans, demonstrating considerable poker-playing skill, told the Honda chief that BMW had made an offer – which he implied was much more attractive than Honda's – and again asked him to raise his bid. Above all, Evans wanted Honda to commit to taking out BAe's remaining 47.5 per cent stake in Rover in five years' time at a guaranteed (and of course acceptable) price. Kawamoto refused to budge. Whether he thought Evans was bluffing or simply would not compromise, or both, the BAe duo did not know. He treated his visitors to a homily about the special relationship between Honda and Rover. But Evans, Simpson and Lapthorne now knew one thing for certain: the chips were down. Either BMW came through, or BAe would be at the mercy of Honda's final terms.

Realizing that he needed something with which to threaten Honda, Simpson had quietly reopened contact with Pischetsrieder. On Sunday 16 January amid enormous secrecy, Alan Curtis, Rover's manufacturing boss, and a colleague flew to Munich to provide the BMW board with the information it needed to table a full bid for Rover. Later that week, Lapthorne met Luderitz. On Wednesday 19 January the BMW board decided to bid and advised BAe the following day of its intention to offer about £700m. Despite their eagerness to rid themselves of Rover, the BAe negotiators steeled themselves and said that £700m would not be enough.

In the ensuing days, BMW continued its due diligence while the sale price, and therefore the sale itself, remained on hold. Finally, at about 5 pm on Wednesday 26 January at the Camomile Street offices of BMW's lawyers Norton Rose, Luderitz formally offered Lapthorne £800m for Rover. After a brief discussion, a further £20m was added to the price, to be paid if Honda stayed on board after the deal rather than instantly pulling out of its contract to provide engines and other components for Rover models, particularly the 600 and 800.

BMW would also take on Rover's average daily debt of £200m and its £700m off-balance-sheet commitments. In total, the offer was worth £1.7bn. BMW set 1 February as the deadline for BAe to make up its mind – on 2 February they said, 'There would be no offer to which BAe would be able to respond.' Eventually, Lapthorne told Luderitz, 'You've got a deal.' Then he, Evans and Simpson worked through the night on their presentation to the full BAe board, which was to meet at the company's London office on Brewer's Green, near St James's Park, the next morning. The directors were unhappy at having to sever the Honda ties and very concerned about the government's reaction.

The Department of Trade and Industry (DTI) was predisposed towards Honda because of the links the government had forged during the 1980s with the Japanese carmakers. The DTI also believed that Britain owed the Japanese a debt. The high productivity transplant factories built by Nissan, Honda and Toyota in Britain had, after all, done more than any other projects to convince foreign firms in other industries that the British economy, once the sick man of Europe, had been revitalized and was now a suitable case for inward investment.

Notwithstanding their reservations, the BAe directors knew an outstanding deal when they saw one. They recognized that, as long as BAe was burdened by Rover's financing requirements, its recovery from the nightmare of 1991–2 could only be partial and painstakingly slow. Liberated from Rover's biannual (January and August were the big car sales months) £1bn funding peaks, which were choking BAe's borrowing capacity, the board believed the company would never look back. The sky would truly be the limit. They approved the sale to BMW, but to

The board believed the company would never look back. The sky would truly be the limit

discharge what they saw as their responsibilities to Honda and to cover the political angle, they dispatched Simpson on his mission to Tokyo to give the Japanese one last chance to match BMW's terms. That left only the British government still to be convinced – and on the issue of the government Pischetsrieder was adamant. 'We would have been very concerned about the reaction of the British public if the government had not backed the deal,' he said. 'The UK is the third largest market for BMW and we cannot afford to have a bad public image in this country.' Evans knew it was not going to be easy. Some days earlier, he and Simpson had been summoned to the DTI after senior officials had picked up rumours that Rover was about to be sold to BMW. Evans decided he had to play his cards very close to his chest. He denied that BAe had reached any agreement to sell Rover which, at the time he said it, was strictly accurate. Outside, on the pavement in Victoria Street, Simpson turned to him. 'I'm not sure I could have done that,' the Rover chief said. 'If I had said any more,' Evans replied, 'they would have killed the deal.'

Now Evans had to go back to the DTI with the news that BAe had indeed agreed the sale of Rover. By coincidence, Michael Heseltine, self-styled president of the Board of Trade and head of the DTI, was out of the country on a trade mission to Asia and Australasia. When contacted by telephone in Hong Kong, where he was staying with the governor-general, Chris Patten, Heseltine was not happy. The following evening, the heat was turned up even higher when Evans and Lapthorne met Tim Sainsbury, Heseltine's deputy.

After the meeting, at BAe's Filton factory near Sainsbury's Bristol constituency, Sainsbury was to dine with the BAe people, together with Pischetsrieder and Luderitz, who would explain where BMW was coming from. First, however, Evans had to take heavy flak from the DTI top brass, who had been advised (misguidedly as it turned out) by the British ambassador in Tokyo that further Japanese investment in Britain would be jeopardized if BAe went ahead. It was even intimated by the DTI people that Evans's career prospects would not be enhanced if he insisted on proceeding with the sale to BMW. But Evans stood firm: he knew that his fundamental duty was to his long-suffering shareholders, and he also knew that the shareholder value of the deal was immense. That was that. Evans and Lapthorne diplomatically skipped the dinner: 'By then, the DTI had probably seen enough of us and we had certainly seen enough of them,' Evans said.

So the burden of persuasion fell on Pischetsrieder. Initially, Sainsbury was sceptical about BMW and sympathetic to Honda. But the BMW chief argued that, if Rover were controlled by a minority shareholder that was able to dictate its profits (by controlling output), then it would always be unattractive to private investors, making the float the government desired unrealistic. He also emphasized the heavy financial commitment BMW would be making to Rover. Sainsbury was won over and Heseltine, when contacted, also came round. Simpson, meanwhile, had finished his business in Tokyo and was flying back to London. He landed at Heathrow at 4 pm on Saturday and met Evans and Lapthorne. The contingent, together with their wives, then flew to Munich and were driven to The Residenz, an exclusive hotel in Aschau, a village in the upper Bavarian mountains where, over drinks and dinner with Pischetsrieder, the deal was signed at 11 pm that night.

Only the details now remained. On Sunday, Simpson and the BMW chief flew to meet the board at Rover's head office near Birmingham international airport, then down to BAe's headquarters at Farnborough. They planned to announce the deal on Monday afternoon, but a leak in Japan forced the news out early on Monday morning and Rover had to bring forward its announcement. After almost eight months of intense negotiation Pischetsrieder had won his prize. And almost 90 years after William Morris had begun making cars at Longbridge, Rover, the last British-owned motor manufacturer, had fallen under foreign control. Pischet-srieder insisted that BMW was in for the long haul and stated that they were not after a short-term dividend. 'If we wanted that, we would have put the money in the bank,' he said.

Everything we now know about BMW's disastrous involvement with Rover suggests that Pischetsrieder was genuine in his analysis that BMW had stolen a march on its rivals. He really did believe that the acquisition of Rover was the answer to BMW's strategic imperative of expansion.

In the early 1990s the received wisdom in the automotive industry was that no auto producer could survive independently without a unit output of at least 1.8m to 2m cars. Less than that and economies of scale, in both production and purchasing, could not be achieved and the company would decline into uncompetitiveness. Also, BMW's de facto owners, the Quandt family, were obsessed with retaining autonomy and independence and to stay independent only three options were open to the BMW chief. First, protect the niche market; second, expand by creating a new brand similar to the manner in which Toyota had created Lexus; third, acquire a ready-made mass producer.

BMW had already concluded that the first was not feasible. The second was rejected on the grounds that establishing a new brand consciousness would take too long and cost too much – Lexus was reckoned to have cost Toyota about $5bn, including product and dealer network creation and brand promotion. Given the increasingly powerful competition in the premium market, BMW would be particularly vulnerable during the time it would take to build a brand from scratch.

The rejection of options one and two left only the third. Pischetsrieder said later that Rover was 'the only alternative left in terms of size, suggested or perceived price and presence in the necessary market areas, geographi-cally as well as in terms of market segmentation'. He concluded that in a hostile environment 'if you want to catch a lion you go into his cave while he's asleep – you don't wait for him to surprise you'.

The acquisition of Rover, therefore, fulfilled both the strategic imper-ative of expansion and the tactical imperative of surprise. As the deal was done it looked as if Pischetsrieder had pulled off a triumph. The German company had almost £1bn in net cash and easy access to the stock and financial markets, so funding an acquisition was not a problem. At the time, Britain and Rover seemed jointly to represent an ideal investment opportunity. The British economy was continuing to grow steadily, with unemployment falling and a corporate sector with greatly improved profitability so Rover seemed to provide the ideal platform for BMW's strategy of expanding to manufacture a full range of upmarket vehicles.

Ironically, Pischetsrieder's grand design completed the strategy that had driven Rover's ostensible revival in the late 1980s. Under Sir Graham Day, then chairman, and Simpson, Rover had attempted to position itself at the upper end of each market segment. The strategy was widely seen as having been modelled on that of BMW itself. A curiously self-perpetuating analysis had begun to dominate the mindsets at the Munich headquarters, so-called because of its structure of four rounded towers the 'four cylinder'. *Independence* was the goal, *expansion* was the strategy and *acquiring Rover* was the tactic. Everything was set fair. They convinced themselves that they had pulled off a coup. In hindsight perhaps it was BAe which had pulled off the coup.

Everything was set fair. They convinced themselves that they had pulled off a coup. In hindsight perhaps it was BAe which had pulled off the coup

PART TWO

Strategy Without Reality

O N 19 MARCH 1994, when John Towers walked into work on the day after BMW formally completed its acquisition of Rover, he could have been forgiven for not noticing very much difference from life under British Aerospace. Towers did, of course, soon see considerable changes, but surely not in the way he or anyone else would have expected. Instead of being surrounded by a crowd of BMW executives, Towers found the only obvious changes were that his salary would soon be virtually doubled and Rover would be awash with the money everyone had been saying was the only missing ingredient in its efforts to establish itself upmarket.

Towers has since admitted that had he been in Pischetsrieder's shoes he would have installed his own people more quickly. Towers fully expected to be the transition man and then to go. 'If you look through the history of these sort of marriages then you don't need that many people in the business who think they're running the business. Particularly with takeovers from overseas you end up putting your own people in anyway,' he said. Towers saw his role as primarily to ensure that 'we managed a successful transition away from the Honda relationship without any chasms occurring as part of that'. Although, inexplicably, Pischetsrieder genuinely appeared to want a British CEO in place, de facto Towers was from the start only the 'transition man'. As Towers said, 'It was no coincidence that I left as soon as the last major Honda programme [Rover 400] was completed.'

Since BAe's financial crisis, Rover had limped along with annual investment of no more than £200m – barely enough to keep the operation turning over. Much of the talk in the final days of BAe's ownership was that the £450m a year of investment promised by BMW would cure all Rover's ills. Those ills were not deemed to be the fault of Towers, the board, the strategy or even the oft-maligned workforce – the ills were simply a consequence of under-investment.

Notwithstanding the general euphoria, at least one senior BAe executive warned Pischetsrieder that such an analysis was way off the mark and that Towers was, in fact, part of the problem rather than the solution. Imagine that executive's surprise when, in one of his first actions as Rover's new chairman, Pischetsrieder chose to double Towers's salary. Towers was probably just as surprised. The consequence of such a pay rise was, however, that Towers was to have his management talents truly tested. Lack of investment is often an easy get-out for ineffective management, but when the investment arrives, as it did from BMW, there is no hiding place.

Lack of investment is often an easy get-out for ineffective management, but when the investment arrives, as it did from BMW, there is no hiding place

The only sensible explanation behind Pischetsrieder's apparent inactivity during the period immediately after the takeover was a belief that the production processes and working culture of Rover could best be reoriented by a largely hands-off managerial approach during which German practices would be gradually absorbed by the British, predominantly as the result of some sort of educational osmosis. Pischetsrieder consciously resisted the desire of some of his colleagues in BMW to, as one put it with Bavarian indelicacy, 'tell those buggers in Britain what to do and that's it'. Although Pischetsrieder's hands-off approach was deliberate policy by the BMW chief, it was also a result of the constraints BMW felt obliged to acknowledge because of what it saw as the political and cultural sensitivities of the takeover.

Despite having talked Heseltine and his colleagues into the idea of the Rover purchase, BMW executives remained acutely aware of the pro-Honda feeling in the Department of Trade and Industry. The cloak-and-dagger secrecy in which BAe and BMW had conducted the negotiations had left its mark: Pischetsrieder and his cohorts felt that if they were seen to be trampling all over Rover then they would suffer a backlash that would harm not only their plan to revitalize the British marque, but could also badly damage BMW's image in Britain – the largest and most profitable market for BMW cars after Germany and the USA.

Pischetsrieder and his team knew that, at best, BMW faced a long and delicate process in transforming Rover into a premium marque. At the outset, the day after the deal was announced, Pischetsrieder told the media that Rover would not be profitable until 2000 and that it would take eight years before they had completed the planned transformation. That was a classic instance of a chief executive buying himself time – but it may actually have reflected an understatement of the undoubted reality.

At the time, Pischetsrieder's profit outlook seemed to be excessively cautious: according to BAe's figures, Rover was heading back into profit after losing £9m before tax in 1993. However, BMW had much more rigorous accounting standards – one Rover manager joked that if top British companies applied the same criteria as BMW then hardly anyone would show a profit. BMW was, for example, particularly severe in its treatment of depreciation, a fact that compounded the impact on Rover's cash flow of the huge increase in investment. Cash was soon pouring out of the business.

Nor could BMW expect to enhance Rover's margins easily by raising its prices to levels commensurate with those of a premium marque. Rover, despite its advertising campaign pretensions and aspirations to be the British BMW, was not in the same league as the Bavarians. After years of under-investment and colonization by Honda, it had an enormous amount of ground to cover before consumers would be prepared to pay premium prices for its products.

A further factor conditioning BMW's hands-off approach was the Germans' lack of familiarity with Britain as a production base. This in turn reflected the insularity of the Munich company, which owned only two factories outside Bavaria – a long-established plant in South Africa and the Spartanburg site in South Carolina, which was just being completed. The result was that BMW took the completely opposite approach to that adopted by Ford after its £1.6bn acquisition of Jaguar in 1989.

While taking care to keep most of Jaguar's top management British, Ford rapidly replaced Jaguar's chairman, Sir John Egan, with its own man, Bill Hayden. Hayden, with a hand-picked few experts from Ford, then embarked on a course of shock treatment and intense therapy for the existing Jaguar management. Many found the experience extremely painful, but most recognized later that Hayden had saved the business. By the time that Hayden handed over to his successor, Nick Scheele, four years after the takeover Jaguar was on new solid foundations for recovery and growth.

Like Ford, BMW had wanted to take a short cut that would leave the competition trailing. Ford wanted to save the time and money-consuming process of growing its own luxury marque from scratch. But Jaguar was not an instant success. In fact, in 1991 Ford almost closed down the Coventry company. Yet by 1995 it was in the process of trebling the size of the company with a new car and a £400m factory creating several thousand jobs. Most of the numbers were against Jaguar. Ford had itself to blame for buying the company at such a huge price. It was so determined to see off Jaguar's preferred partner, General Motors, that it paid over the odds. Among executives in the Glasshouse, Ford's glass-fronted, high-rise head office in the Dearborn suburb of Detroit, Jaguar caught the backlash.

This was understandable, considering that until the fourth quarter of 1999 Jaguar had barely made a penny of profit for Ford. At one stage Jaguar's deficit over the six years since the takeover totalled £760m. Every set of figures carried the scars of the acquisition: not only was Ford having to write off £1.3bn of goodwill since Jaguar's net assets had totalled only £300m, but the early 1990s recession, the fall in the dollar and the slump in American demand for European luxury cars piled up the losses. On top of that, Jaguar's reputation for quality had been battered by the unreliability of its XJ40 saloon. In the 1992 survey of car customer satisfaction by the highly respected JDPower organization in America, Jaguar suffered the indignity of being ranked twenty-fifth, beating only the South Korean company, Hyundai.

The crunch came in 1992. Harold 'Red' Poling, chairman, and Alex Trotman, his heir apparent, considered cutting their losses and closing down Jaguar. The big cat was saved by the Ford family: William Clay Ford, Henry's great-grandson and father of Ford's current chairman, was a Jaguar devotee who had owned a Jaguar since his college days. He believed that the marque could be revived. Ford is, ultimately, a family-controlled company. Jaguar stayed in business.

In autumn 1993, when he hosted Ford's annual dinner in London for its leading British suppliers, Trotman confessed that Jaguar was his biggest problem. In fact, while the headline losses did not show it, Jaguar's turnaround was already under way. Hayden had slashed the 12,800 workforce to 7000, improved quality and removed archaic working practices. Just as crucially for the company's brand image, Hayden had resisted the attempts by some zealous Ford executives to 'Fordize' Jaguar completely, an impulse reinforced by the company's plunge into the red.

The biggest battle came over whether Jaguar should get its own engine for its planned new XJ6 saloon and XK8 sports model. Some Dearborn people wanted to force an off-the-shelf Ford engine down the big cat's throat. Jaguar successfully resisted, again thanks to support from Bill Ford senior. The result was a happy compromise: a Jaguar-designed engine, the AJ26, to be made at Ford's Bridgend plant. Scheele, who succeeded Hayden, cut the workforce further, to 6000, and continued Hayden's efficiency and quality drive so successfully that productivity more than doubled in six years.

But in product terms, all the focus was on the new saloon. If that failed, Scheele knew, Jaguar's hopes of winning Ford backing for a new mid-sized saloon, which became the S-type, would be dead. By rigorously focusing all his resources on the job in hand, Scheele built up the confidence of his bosses in America and ultimately won the go-ahead for the S-type. In the end, it probably cost Ford as much to get Jaguar in shape as it would have done had the company grown its own luxury brand. However, what Ford could not have grown was the value of the Jaguar symbol once it was attached to the bonnet of some high-quality cars. The contrast with BMW and Rover is instructive and, for BMW, stark.

Pischetsrieder was aware of the parallels: once, early in the Rover ownership, he was asked what Rovers should be. 'Cheap Jaguars,' he replied. The problem was that BMW drew only positive messages from Ford's experience – the feeling that Rover could emulate Jaguar – without recognizing that the real lessons were in fact negative. Despite its honourable post-war heritage, Rover could not compete with the strength of the Jaguar brand. For Jaguar, the residual halo effect of the iconographic E-type and the afficionados' love for the stylish Mark II signified a dormant brand, not a dying one. The big cat marque had never lost the goodwill of its customers. Even the British company executives who began to desert when quality plummeted in the late 1980s knew exactly what the brand stood for and were simply waiting for the product to catch up with the brand once more. The reason they began to buy Mercedes, BMW and Lexus was because the then-new XJ40 saloon, the last product of Egan's regime, fell far short of what they expected a Jaguar to be – it just wasn't a Jaguar. In stark contrast, the Viking longship had lost its identity during its depersonalized decades under the tattered British Leyland emblem. Those who remembered what Rover was, when it could look Jaguar in the eye in the 1950s and 1960s, formed an ever-dwindling minority of the car-buying public. The collective memory had faded fast.

When Pischets-rieder revealed the planned takeover to his senior managers, they gave him a rapturous reception. But as time passed the mood slowly darkened

Ironically, and partly because Rover was seen to have lost its way, many industry insiders, who had been the biggest worriers that Ford would ruin Jaguar, took the view that BMW's purchase of Rover was by far the best thing that could have happened to the British company. Their justification for such a view was that Rover would now get a thorough grounding in BMW's renowned engineering and marketing skills. The deal was also warmly received at the Four Cylinder in Munich. When Pischetsrieder revealed the planned takeover to his senior managers, they gave him a rapturous reception. But as time passed after completion of the purchase, the mood slowly darkened. An increasing number of managers back in Munich and some frustrated younger managers at Rover became increasingly bemused by the softly-softly approach adopted by the BMW hierarchy. Rover's management and culture were effectively left virtually undisturbed for almost two years. The time wasted during that period was probably more damaging even than the expense BMW incurred as it poured money into Rover with little obvious return.

Pischetsrieder was, no doubt, mindful of the case lore of corporate transactions. More fail than succeed, according to several studies, and the cultural difficulties experienced before, during and after mergers and acquisitions are well documented. The Anglophile Pischetsrieder prided himself on an empathetic understanding of the British automobile industry and its heritage. He reasoned that an abrupt change in working practices and managerial style would be resisted and consequently would be counter-productive.

In this, as in other areas, BMW probably outsmarted itself. What was most odd about the situation was that it paid little attention to the need for a 'reality audit' prior to the establishment of a strategic direction. As a consequence, even before the dust had settled on the takeover, Pischetsrieder was making statements and policies which would later come to haunt him. For example, he said, 'We mustn't create the perception that Rover was only the puppet on BMW strings.' He was intent therefore on 'sharpening the BMW identity while building a completely different Rover identity'.

Such a strategy, Pischetsrieder argued, would mean that the lower margins of a volume producer need not necessarily concern the new Rover since it would not 'aim for the mass market'. Instead it would pursue the 'creaming off' strategy which targeted the top end of each and every market segment. According to BMW's market analysis, only 20 per cent of consumers in the premium segment worldwide would consider buying a BMW. The other 80 per cent were not attracted to the sporty, dynamic driver's car image of the ultimate driving machine.

Rover was to be something different. With the accent on comfort and refinement, it was to be the ultimate motoring machine – a brand which enabled BMW to tap part of that 80 per cent who favoured brands other than BMW. Volvo was seen as a particular rival, as was Audi. And, of course, Rovers could be smaller than BMWs – opening up a new segment below the 3-series. 'Rovers should be cars of a special character, cars that won't please the majority but will please a large minority,' Pischetsrieder told *Car* magazine two years later:

> ❝ They should be cars with a consistent message. BMWs have had a consistent message for a long time – that's why our image is very precise. Rovers can occupy mainstream sectors, such as the Golf class – unlike BMW – and yet still have exclusivity. That's not a niche, it's too big for a niche. Rather, it's a very strong marketing opportunity ❞.

This approach would compensate for lower British sales – as the brand was extracted from the volume sector, which BMW planners called 'die rationale Wuste' (the 'rational desert') – with increased exports, particularly to the continent. In this way the strategy would effectively subvert the 'niche' versus 'mass' marketing debate by turning a collection of niches into a volume market.

As Pischetsrieder explained, 'I have a vision of this new group [BMW/Rover] being in so many markets that it can serve many more niches than any of the traditional mass-market manufacturers.' Martin Runnacles, who at the time was marketing manager for BMW (GB), was also reluctant to use the term 'niche', preferring to think of the group 'working within volume markets, but in a new kind of way'. Even the high priest of brand power, Reitzle, then BMW's director of research and development, explained that the acquisition of Rover meant that the BMW brand did not have to be 'stretched too much, [which] would not be as perfect from a marketing viewpoint'. However, such a view had not prevented Reitzle from developing a 2-series model that was almost ready to take its place in the BMW portfolio.

Interlinked with the marketing and investment strategy was a manufacturing strategy aimed at boosting productivity, which Pischetsrieder claimed was 50 per cent lower than in BMW's Bavarian plants. Much later, BMW executives eventually admitted some regret at not defining more precisely what they had meant. Pischetsrieder has since said it had 'nothing to do with output per head', which he called 'a rather suspicious figure'. Rather it was much more to do with a more holistic view, more akin to a balanced scorecard approach, in which productivity means added value per paid hour. Raising productivity defined in this way meant that the expensive equipment BMW planned to put into Rover would have to be run virtually round the clock. This would mean huge working practice changes – another obstacle to be overcome in due course.

However, both the branding and the managerial strategies were predicated on Pischetsrieder's perception of reality as it existed at the time of acquisition. Was that perception correct? With hindsight, clearly not. But is it reasonable for Pischetsrieder to be blamed, in hindsight? Possibly not.

As an example of the difficulties of prediction, an article at the time, in *Financial World* (24 May 1994), painted a very enthusiastic picture of the future for both BMW and Rover. Of course, the author of that piece did not have to live with the consequences of his judgement, whereas Pischet-srieder did. How accurate, then, was the Pischetsrieder reality?

The Company

BMW found a company whose car range had, ever-increasingly over almost 15 years, been kept afloat by the European strategy of Honda. Apart from Rover's innovative K-series engine, which powered the smaller models and had been developed with Bhattacharyya's Warwick Manufacturing Group, the Japanese had provided the majority of the technology that had revived Rover's product range and, of course, its processes and factories. BMW also found a company which had been in decline for many years, notwithstanding the apparent revival just before the takeover. Day had taken a calculated risk in 1986 when he applied the Rover name to the whole of the cars range. Dropping the Austin name helped the smaller cars, but it badly diluted Rover's image as an executive carmaker. Ultimately, the whole Rover marque was devalued as a result.

Lack of cash and poor management at many levels had meant that the wrong cars had been made (albeit with gradually fewer faults) in too many ranges. The models had been incapable of substantiating the marketing claims made for them, so that Rover lacked credibility with the consumer. In demanding premium prices for its product, it was trying to run before it could walk. To mix a metaphor or two, because of its lack of investment resources, it was also trying to make bricks without straw.

BMW quickly realized that Rover cars was essentially a rump operation, the result of the domino collapse of seven brands and the sale of Jaguar which had all occurred since the ill-conceived birth of British Leyland in 1968. The stark truth was that, at the time of the takeover, Rover maintained twice as many car platforms as BMW, spread over similar volume but with lower prices and minimal margins. Rover also probably had more excess capacity than BMW could possibly have utilized in ten years.

Only the Honda connection had been making Rover at least minimally viable. In terms of manufacturing – discipline, attention to detail, production quality – Rover cars had learned a lot from the Japanese. But for BMW, even the Honda influence on Rover was a mixed blessing. Unlike the Japanese with their emphasis on 'kaizen' – continuous improvement – the German manufacturing bible laid down hard and fast rules for what constituted premium quality. The Ronda [as jokers labelled the Honda-ized Rover] way was to inculcate a culture of quality into each and every process, including management, rather than simply by increasing inspections. This approach was perceived as incompatible with typical German industrial culture. The story that Mercedes had more inspectors than Lexus had workers to make its cars may have been apocryphal, but it illustrated a cultural divide that would not be easy to bridge. To a certain extent, therefore, even the good news – a refocused workforce – may have been bad news for a BMW determined not to interfere.

Even more significant was the fact that the good news of more enlightened management and efficient processes had managed to obscure the underlying bad news of a dying brand. So, BMW found that it had bought a company with deep-seated problems. Yet, bubbling with the self-confidence bred of their company's own remarkable turnaround from near disaster, plus the outstanding growth of the BMW brand, the Bavarians saw Rover as a glass one-quarter full rather than three-quarters empty.

Pischetsrieder and Luderitz viewed the deal as getting Land Rover and a cars marque complementary to BMW, plus Mini and MG, for the £800m price of developing a single model. A more appropriate way of looking at the deal would have been as a balance sheet, with the assets of Land Rover, Mini and MG offset by the liability that was Rover cars – much as the profits made by Land Rover had been continually cancelled out by the cars' losses. That approach would have generated one very simple but critical question: would the good drive out the bad, or would the bad drag down the good? It was a question that Pischetsrieder and his colleagues never seem to have asked themselves. In order to secure the purchase they had convinced themselves that the former was true and the picture as rosy as that painted by *Financial World.*

The Environment

The same level of self-deception was evident in relation to the automotive industry as a whole. The environment in which the new company was expected to operate was not particularly welcoming. In the year leading up to the acquisition of Rover the western European market had declined by 16 per cent in volume. Volkswagen lost close to £1bn, Fiat also lost money and was operating at only just over 50 per cent of capacity, Ford was losing money and Renault and Peugeot were also experiencing difficulties. Renault's problems were linked to the collapse of its merger with Volvo and Peugeot was banking on joint projects with Fiat to refresh its fortunes: all this destabilizing activity in a market with surplus capacity approaching 2m units in 1993. Again, Pischetsrieder saw this as a plus, not a minus. BMW was in better shape than most and was, he reasoned, able to steal a march on rivals – such as Ford and Fiat – which might also have considered buying Rover if they had not been preoccupied with their own problems. But while competitors' travails left BMW with a clear run at Rover, the pressures on profitability meant BMW would be trying to resuscitate Rover in a cold climate. As if such overcapacity were not bad enough, all the European carmakers were becoming more efficient, adding to the problem. Additionally, Japanese transplants in the UK were building towards an eventual capacity close to 1m cars by the start of the new millennium. Nissan's tremendous success in Sunderland was yet another bad indicator for inefficient companies.

An obvious outlet for this overcapacity was the American market, which Pischetsrieder looked to initially, especially for the Land Rover brand. The United States had been an immensely lucrative hunting

> **In the year leading up to the acquisition of Rover the western European market had declined by 16 per cent in volume**

ground for BMW in the 1980s. BMW sales in the USA had peaked in 1986 at 97,000 units. But in 1991, hit by the recession, the weak dollar and strong competition from Honda's Acura and Toyota's Lexus, sales nosedived to 57,000. BMW had responded to these horrendous figures by reducing prices, starting a new 3-series and building a new plant on a green-field site at Spartanburg in South Carolina. After teething troubles, the American factory has earned its keep, enabling BMW to avoid diluting its 'made in Germany' image. Spartanburg's BMWs have managed to maintain the aura of German engineering excellence.

In the two years leading up to the Rover acquisition, BMW's marketing drive in the USA had first arrested and then reversed the sales decline up to 1991. Mercedes had similarly halted its decline and followed BMW's lead by building a plant in Tuscaloosa, Alabama. Pischetsrieder and Reitzle immediately looked to America for the Land Rover brand which they considered under-exploited in the USA, and in the longer term for Rover cars, Mini and MG. The main driver of Land Rover sales, in America and elsewhere, was the Discovery, whose worldwide sales peaked at 70,000 in the year of the BMW acquisition – more than half the Land Rover total. Discovery had significant quality problems which were triggering hefty warranty payments. These had prompted a standing joke in the industry.

Q: What are the two man-made structures visible from outer space?

A: The Great Wall of China and the shut lines on the Discovery.

Such problems would have destroyed sales of Rover cars, but again the power of a brand came to the rescue. The strength and desirability of the Land Rover brand was sufficient to override such problems. Anything that would expand the Land Rover range and tap into this demand was of acute interest to the operation's new owners.

Pischetsrieder and Reitzle were, therefore, delighted when, the day after the takeover was announced, they visited Rover's Gaydon development centre and were shown a prototype of a small four-by-four, which was to become the Freelander. There was, of course, a hitch: to save money, the cash-strapped Rover had formed a 50–50 joint venture with the Finnish company Valmet under which Valmet (which was also to make the

Porsche Boxster) was to fund and manufacture the Freelander body before shipping it to Solihull for completion. In return, Valmet would get half the profits on the vehicle. The arrangement was similar to that concluded by Rover cars with the engineering group Mayflower to make the forthcoming MGF sportscar. But while it was too late to cancel the Mayflower deal, BMW immediately took steps to withdraw from the Valmet contract. Freelander was reborn as a 100 per cent Land Rover venture and proved a huge success when it was launched in 1996. Even here, however, BMW allowed Rover to make one big mistake. To save money, Freelander was not 'homologated' (engineered) to comply with US safety and environmental regulations, so it could not be sold in America, potentially its largest market. The error was only rectified five years later, so that Freelander would finally enter the US market in 2001.

As with the state of Rover, BMW had convinced themselves that the state of the environment was conducive to an acquisition which, although it appeared clever, was decidedly risky – to put it mildly.

CHAPTER 4

The Challenges

T HE CHALLENGES thrown up by the state of Rover and the automotive
environment were formidable and complexly interrelated. There
were challenges with the *people*, the *processes* and the *brand*.

People

The 'people' challenges subdivided into those concerning management
and those concerning the workforce. At the very top there was the potentially disruptive influence of the incumbent managing director, John
Towers. It was common knowledge that Towers had favoured a continuation of the close ties with Honda in the event of a sale by BAe. He may
even have expected an equity stake in Rover and, despite his huge pay rise,
it was clear that Towers did not take kindly to being an employee of a mid-
range German company as opposed to the boss of a major British industrial player.

The challenge which Pischetsrieder had inherited was not only a
management team close to Honda but one which, with two exceptions –
Alan Curtis, the manufacturing chief and Tony Rose, finance director –
had been excluded from any of the negotiations with BMW precisely
because it was so close to Honda. Those negotiations had been left
primarily in the hands of George Simpson, Rover's chairman, who had
already secured his own exit strategy with a move to the Lucas group. Any
management team would be feeling fragile by such a turn of events and
Pischetsrieder was left with the classic 'purge or persuade' dilemma. He
chose to persuade.

Ironically, for 'sons of British Leyland' the workforce would not prove to be as much of a challenge as the management. Over the years, Simpson, his personnel director Rob Meakin, Towers and some other key executives had completed the hard work in erasing the memory of 'Red Robbo'. Generally the working practices were adequate if not excellent. In Tony Woodley the Transport and General Workers Union (T&GWU) had an automotive industry negotiator of genuinely high calibre. Woodley, a 'scouser', was tough but realistic. He had made his way in the union world in the turbulent and conflictual days of the 1970s and 1980s. He had seen the unions decimated and all but emasculated during the Thatcher era and was probably a better negotiator for the experience. The same could not be said for many of the local convenors with whom Woodley and BMW both had difficulties. Unlike with management, Pischetsrieder did not have the choice of 'purging' the workforce, he had to persuade. Where he did have a choice, however, was in whether to achieve the persuasion by a hands-on or hands-off approach. He chose 'hands off'.

Processes

The reality of the inadequacy of the capital assets should have been apparent to everybody, but again it was seemingly suppressed by the adrenalin of the acquisition. Overshadowing everything was the 90-year-old bottomless pit known as Longbridge. When Herbert Austin began making cars at the disused printing works in 1905, it is doubtful whether even he would have expected it to have survived into the next millennium. Professor Dan Jones, co-author of the influential book, *The Machine That Changed the World*, said in May 2000 that 'Longbridge is a hell-hole – given the choice you wouldn't start from there'. This comment is precisely echoed one by Manfred Schoch, deputy chairman of the BMW super-visory board, about a year earlier. Schoch said that BMW had always been reluctant to build on either brown-field sites or convert existing urban sites: 'We looked at the success of Spartanburg and worried about Longbridge, we wouldn't have gone for Longbridge out of choice,' he said.

Longbridge's problem was covering its overhead. It had been producing below its capacity – between 450,000 and 500,000 units a year – for many years. The Longbridge headache was intimately related to the gaps in Rover's product line – in particular, its failure to replace the Metro, which despite being renamed and facelifted was finding it increasingly difficult to disguise that fact that it was more than 15 years old.

No carmaker made much money from its supermini range – the 'B' class, in British market definitions – but all of them relied on the high volumes from such models to generate cash to fund the more profitable larger segments. The Simpson regime had recognized Rover's problem.

Since BAe's financial crisis meant Rover had no chance of completely funding a new supermini, Simpson had explored alternatives. Consideration was given to borrowing a city car platform from Honda. But Simpson also held discussions with Ford about a model swap that would have enabled Rover to use Ford's Ka platform to develop a new B-class car, while giving Ford the Rover 800 platform to replace the fast-fading Scorpio. Ford was receptive to the idea, but the discussions were overtaken by BAe's desperation to sell Rover.

In volume terms, a yawning gap opened up between the 200 and the ageing 100 and Mini – and Longbridge was caught right in the middle of it

Rover was left to make a virtue out of necessity by arguing that its move upmarket meant that its future offerings would be positioned at the top end of each segment. The first, out in 1995, was the 400. It was followed by the new 200. But with the size–price ratio of the 400 straddling the C and D segments, and that of the 200 uncomfortably bridging the B and C classes, the failure to develop a fully fledged new supermini pushed Rover's product line out of synch with the British and mainland European market. In volume terms, a yawning gap opened up between the 200 and the ageing 100 and Mini – and Longbridge was caught right in the middle of it.

BMW was left with three choices over Longbridge and Rover's smaller car product line: first, keep going as it was until a new range could be introduced to replace the 200 and 400; second, prune the site drastically; third, make BMWs in Longbridge. Some experts believed that the first course could be financially ruinous and take years to effect. They therefore advocated cutting back – or even closing – Longbridge, or building 3-series cars at the plant. The trouble was that both these options were complete anathema to Pischetsrieder's plan for Rover. To keep faith with the British government and retain the hearts and minds of Rover employees and Rover and BMW customers in Britain, he believed redundancies were out of the question.

The whole of the European traditional industry sector, and it is particularly true in Britain, is dogged by the political necessity to retain jobs in mono-industry regions. The legacy of the mine and steel closures and the decimation of communities was, at that time, still fresh in the political memories of both John Major's languishing Conservative party and New Labour's 'wannabee' government. Pischetsrieder admitted being sensitive to such considerations:

> We knew this was a sensitive area, but I think we thoroughly investigated whether a corporate policy for the new company would comply with the national interests in the UK. For example, we never considered forcing Rover plants to make BMW cars, even if it made sense from a bottom-line point of view. That would have caused a major outcry in the UK, our third largest market, and obviously would have harmed our BMW business there. (CHIEF EXECUTIVE, OCTOBER 94)

There was another constraint. Since Pischetsrieder's whole motivation for the takeover was to preserve BMW's exclusivity, while increasing the size of the group, in order to give it critical mass, he would not contemplate mixed manufacture at a common site. So, even at the risk to the bottom line, Pischetsrieder was prepared to take on the burden of Longbridge rather than face the political fall-out from a closure that many analysts expected. The result was that, right from the outset, the Longbridge issue was a boil that was festering rather than being lanced. There was only one potentially disastrous process challenge and that was Longbridge. Pischetsrieder effectively ducked the challenge.

Brand

Shortly after his dramatic departure from BMW in February 1999, Reitzle said:

> 66 In the future [the auto business] will be a power game with brands, the product will always be at the core – but not the dominating factor that it was in the past. The importance of sales and marketing in the next decade will be even greater than in the last 10 years. The products are increasingly at a similar level of quality. There are almost no bad cases on the market; even for mass-produced products, quality is now a given, not a matter of differentiation 99.

His statement should not have come as a surprise since it had been his view throughout the period of the Rover ownership and indeed prior to the acquisition. However, it is doubtful if even Reitzle appreciated the depths to which the Rover brand had plunged. Rover had been sick for many years and only its largely export successes in France and Italy had maintained any semblance of brand viability. BMW's concern was how much elasticity existed in their brand and how best could that elasticity be used in relation to Rover? It was the classic branding debate which occurs with all mergers and acqusitions (M&As) and one which is, of course, best resolved before the acquisition. Does the appeal of expanding volume outweigh the threat of diluting the predator's brand? It was a debate, often subliminal, which would taint the whole of BMW's ownership of Rover.

At the outset Pischetsrieder made it absolutely clear that the brands would remain separate. 'The independent management of both brands,' he said, 'is the most important pre-requisite for success of this new deal. It is our objective to guide two independent and powerful automobile manufacturers on a common route through the future in a competitive world market' (*Marketing Week*, 4 February 1994). On another occasion he added that the Rover and BMW brands 'supplement each other in an almost ideal manner'. (*Marketing*, 10 February 1994). Pischetsrieder clearly believed that a 2-series BMW, for example, would be stretching the brand too far. He stated that, 'In that particular segment there was an incompatibility between volume and premium; in order to generate volume we would have had to dilute the premium.'

Reitzle's view was markedly different. In a sense, the whole idea of buying into Rover had originated with him. In the early 1990s, on a visit to Japan with von Kuenheim, the two men had fallen to discussing – much as football fans debate their all-star team – the ideal portfolio of premium marques. They came up with four: BMW, of course, was a given. The other three were Porsche, which BMW and Mercedes both subsequently tried to acquire, Rolls-Royce and – Land Rover.

Reitzle thought Rover cars was a brand beyond recall and believed that the only point of acquiring Rover was to gather up its existing premium brands – MG, Land Rover, Mini – and use its volume production capabilities to stretch the BMW brand, which could include a 2-series made in Britain. While Pischetsrieder believed Rover had to complement BMW throughout its range, and should not be reduced to become a maker of cars smaller than the 3-series, Reitzle was desperate to avoid any overlap between the BMW range and Rover.

In Pischetsrieder's words, Reitzle's inclinations were always to 'steer clear of the mass market and much rather acquire a chateau in Bordeaux'. Both brand strategies had merits, but Pischetsrieder's, which relied heavily on the Rover brand making a full recovery from years of illness, was the most vulnerable. This was clear at the time, not just in hindsight. Perhaps the BMW chief could not see the reality through the misty eyes of a buyer's optimism.

5 The Tactic

G IVEN THAT THE STRATEGY for dealing with Rover and the environment was predicated on a disputable understanding of the reality of the situation, it was no surprise that the tactics chosen to realize the strategy and deal with the challenges were less than focused. The first model developed by Rover under BMW ownership, for example, was the replacement for both the Rover 800 and the 600. The decision surprised the industry, which pleased Pischetsrieder because BMW delighted in doing the unexpected. The decision broke Rover's existing product cycle, under which the top-of-the-range Rover 800 was the next model due for replacement. While every commentator had duly anticipated that BMW would stop the 800, no one had foreseen the demise of the newest model, the 600. Pischetsrieder had first signalled publicly that BMW might opt to focus on the upper-medium Rover 600 segment rather than the 800 when he was interviewed by the *Sunday Times* in October 1994:

> ❝ Yes, the Rover 800 is the next car due to be replaced. But the success of BMW has been based on our refusal to do the obvious,' he said. 'When you look at the countless number of competitors who have tried to pull up their marque by launching a top-of-the-range model, you hardly find a single one who has not failed because they didn't have the foundation for it. Using the 600 would provide a volume base for the customers to move up to the 800.' Pischetsrieder added that 'the clear volume objective for Rover is a two- or three-fold increase' ❞.

That implied sales of well over 1m vehicles, including Land Rover. But he also said Rover must go further upmarket. "Rover has to be more exclusive. The question is: what is the best way to achieve that?"

BMW wanted a top-of-the-range model that would exemplify the new Rover values and cast a halo over the smaller cars in the range, as well as increasing Rover's volume. To do that, it needed a model with sufficient presence at the upper end of the market to change consumer perceptions. The 800 segment was too small to allow such an impact. From the outset, BMW planned to sell at least 120,000 of the 600/800 replacement each year, and it hoped for 140,000.

BMW wanted a top-of-the-range model that would exemplify the new Rover values and cast a halo over the smaller cars in the range, as well as increasing Rover's volume

This compared with the 1994 peak of 80,000 units reached by the 600 and 800 combined. Certainly, by the standards of the premium priced segment in which BMW operated and where Pischetsrieder wanted to position Rover, the decision made sense. BMW's engine room is the 3-series, which then, and still more today, generates most of the company's sales and profit. BMW sells almost as many 3-series as Ford sells Mondeos, but what makes consumers willing to pay premium prices for what is a relatively high volume product is the halo cast by the 5- and 7-series. In theory what the 600/800 replacement was supposed to do for Rover's smaller cars was the same as the 5 and 7 did for BMW.

The other factor that was hard at work in motivating the 600 decision was Pischetsrieder's desire to dilute Honda's influence on Rover as quickly as possible, for a combination of reasons both practical and strategic. Apart from everything else, Honda retained a 20 per cent stake in the Rover operating company, which BMW had to buy out before it could take full control. This required delicate manoeuvring, because BMW could not afford to break Rover's links with the Japanese altogether. Honda had the right to stop supplying Rover at three months' notice. Theoretically, then, it could shut Rover down. Although that was unlikely, both because it would have been bad for Honda's image and because Honda's own operation at Swindon depended on the economies of scale obtained from supplying Rover and buying common components, it was a real issue that had to be addressed. Indeed, a secret clause in the Rover deal provided for BAe to get an extra £20m from

BMW if, having used its good offices, the British company helped persuade Honda to stay on board.

One of Pischetsrieder's few managerial successes was to allow Towers to play the key role in building a bridge between BMW and Honda. Intensive talks took place in Tokyo during which Pischetsrieder suggested a triple alliance between the companies. Kawamoto, however, was as determined to remain independent as BMW. In the end, at a final negotiating session in New York, BMW agreed to pay Honda £200m for the 20 per cent holding. In return, Honda agreed to continue supplying Rover for the lifetime of the models concerned – 200, 400, 600, 800 – and to reduce the substantial royalties it derived from each unit sold. Given the pre-eminent importance Pischetsrieder attached to the top-of-range model, the deal was particularly significant for the 600. As we have seen, Honda had exacted from the enfeebled BAe and Rover more control over the 600 than over any previous model. Not only was Rover barred from selling the 600 in the USA, but Honda could dictate even the interior design and styling. As with the 200 and 400, Honda was being paid for the engines and other components that it supplied, plus the royalties.

Pischetsrieder also believed that Rover could never achieve truly premium brand quality and prices unless it got away from what BMW saw as the volume orientated Honda approach. Japanese production quality might be outstanding, but it was engineered, mechanical quality rather than the kind of look, feel and ambience that created a distinctive, exclusive brand. The contrast was embodied in the different production systems. Honda's system of making cars in batches, which Rover was still compelled to use because of its dependence on the Japanese company, also conflicted with BMW's marketing objectives for Rover. BMW builds cars to individual customer order and wanted Rover to do the same, particularly at Cowley, where Rover built the 600 and 800. It was only much later, when Rover began to implode under the impact of its smaller hybrid class cars and the soaring pound, that the flaw in the model strategy became apparent.

By opting to replace the top-of-range model first instead of the middle market cars that generated most of Rover's volume, BMW had put the cart – impressive as the Rover 75 was – ahead of the workhorse. In consumers' eyes, Rover was too close to the volume market to make one bound into the rarefied realms of the premium segment. Experts inside and outside the company argued that BMW should have adopted the strategy that had brought Volkswagen its cachet within the volume sector, and developed a Golf-size model that could have sold in sufficient numbers to keep the

BMW seemed intent on drawing the wrong lessons

whole show on the road while still convincing consumers that it was moving upmarket. The 600 replacement would then have been the icing on the Rover cake, rather than a castle in the air. It has to be said that this argument is often represented as being loaded with the wisdom of hindsight. That is being too easy on BMW. The examples were out there – VW and Ford – but BMW seemed intent on drawing the wrong lessons.

Another questionable element of the strategy was whether keeping the BMW and Rover brands separate was as important as Pischetsrieder obviously considered it to be. Given the huge gulf between the strength of the BMW brand and the weakness of Rover, separating the two brands effectively did nothing for either of them. One motor industry expert in Germany who knew BMW well explained their thinking:

> 66 The problem for BMW in replacing the 800 with a 5-series is that you are beginning to confuse the two brands and that could start to dilute the BMW position. That will not necessarily be the case forever, because Rover can improve its image and then using a BMW design will be more acceptable. But for the moment, they will leave the 800 segment alone and go to the 600 99.

That type of thinking revealed the true problem – a failure to recognize the weakness of the Rover brand. No amount of manoeuvring between the 800 and 600 could have enhanced the Rover brand. VW's ownership of Skoda provided a good example. While it has improved perceptions of Skoda's reliability, it has not substantially altered the status of the brand. Similarly, no matter how wonderful the Rover 75 turned out to be, and it became European Car of the Year, still nobody bought it – except when it was discounted to such an extent that even slim margins disappeared. It was always unlikely that Rover would critically dilute the

BMW brand and it was equally unlikely that BMW could resuscitate the Rover brand. Essentially, that was the stark reality of the position in late 1994 and BMW failed to recognize it.

6 **Dawn Breaks**

BY THE SUMMER OF 1995 the realization of the true situation was beginning to dawn on everyone and rumblings began that BMW was losing patience with its British management. By September 1995 Rover had experienced a 13 per cent slump in sales and performed worse than any carmaker in Europe. For all the hype about Rover's revival, it had become clear to everybody that the car side was a congenital loss maker. It did not control either of the two businesses that could have offset the losses on car sales – finance had been outsourced to NatWest's Lombard division while Unipart had the right to distribute the vehicles until 2002. Distribution was reckoned to make at least £60m profits a year and BMW asked Towers to negotiate an early release from the Unipart agreement. But the talks with Sir John Neill, Unipart's chairman, broke down.

BMW's gamble, that Rover's low manufacturing costs and recent success in increasing overseas sales would minimize the drain on profits until BMW could transform its margins with new models, was seen to be failing. What had been seen by many as a Rover revival had been exposed as smoke and mirrors dressing up of the patient by BAe ready for sale. It was never a revival, only a remission.

So established had the legend of Rover's revival become that it began to be widely printed as fact. Will Hutton's best-selling *The State We're In* bracketed Rover with Marks & Spencer as benchmarks of British business excellence. In hindsight it looks like he was right to bracket them together, albeit in the wrong category. Another tome on the supposed 100 top British firms claimed that, while it took BMW three decades to establish itself as a premium brand carmaker, Rover achieved the same transformation in a few years. The folly of such grandiose claims was becoming embarrassingly obvious. Rover had fundamental problems, which BMW would struggle to solve. Despite the general pessimism, Pischetsrieder still had faith that once the BMW-inspired Rovers started rolling off the lines with the 600 replacement, due late 1996 or early in 1997, he could begin to drive the company towards his ultimate goal: a progressive move out of the volume sector into an exclusive category parallel to that occupied by BMW. However, with Rover's profits slumping, that strategy appeared to have come unstuck.

BMW executives had always viewed Rover's own sales forecasts with a healthy scepticism. At the time of the original deal, the one major piece of analysis where BMW had diverged with Rover was over what the Germans' felt were wildly over-optimistic five-year sales forecasts. Suddenly, Munich realised the depth of the problem when BMW executives were presented with Rover's figures for the first seven months of 1995. Rover's European sales (including Britain) slumped by 12.7 per cent to fewer than 190,000 vehicles, the worst performance by any carmaker. The underlying picture was even worse, because sales of the Discovery and new Range Rover, launched in late 1994, were actually up. In Britain, Rover sales in the first seven months were down 11.5 per cent, leaving it with a market share of 11.4 per cent. The share held by Rover cars, excluding Land Rover products, was running in single figures.

Rover's share of the market had been declining for years. Under Sir Graham Day, in the mid-to-late 1980s, Rover had pursued a strategy of moving into the higher margin, upper end of each market segment, arguing that this made market share less important. However, Rover insiders had always privately acknowledged that there was a limit beyond which it would be dangerous for market share to fall. A single-figure share was widely seen as below that limit. Rover's response to the problems was to point out that a big element of the sales decline was the ending of Maestro and Montego production which reduced sales by about 5500 in the first half of the year. However, that did not account for the year-on-year sales falls which almost the entire car range had suffered, including the Rover 600, widely regarded at the time as the best model in the stable. The only exception to the trend was the Rover 400, which was replaced in April with a new version. But even there, the fillip to the company's performance was weaker than Rover had hoped, due at least in part to competition from the Civic, the sister model made by Honda. The Japanese company had learned the lessons of its bruising experience two years earlier, when Rover captured the high ground with the 600 even though the Honda counterpart, the Accord, had been first into the market.

Rover countered that it had to date only introduced the five-door part of the 400 range, with the four-door booted version not due until March 1996, and with two-litre petrol and diesel engined versions still to come. But that was a feeble response to the fierce criticism levelled at the 400. Some commentators said that Rover mistargeted the 400. *Car* magazine (September 1995) argued that consumers were being asked to pay Ford Mondeo prices for what, it said, was really an Escort-class rival. Naturally Rover dismissed the charge. A Rover director said, 'When the model range is complete, people will see that it is a nonsense to say that the marketing is wrong.' He was referring to the launch, planned for December, of the new 200, the last of the Honda-derived cars. The 200, which was planned to go on sale in January 1996, was crucial to BMW's attempts to stem the sales decline of Rover. The current model had been Rover's biggest seller and the company was optimistic that its successor would not only cover the existing 200 market, but also compensate for its weakness in the smaller 'supermini' segment.

The share held by Rover was running in single figures

This was just another example of wishful thinking. Rover was drifting worryingly in other ways. The group workforce had actually increased over the previous two years, to 36,000, primarily due to recruitment at Land Rover as Solihull expanded. But Longbridge still employed about 18,000 and Rover's productivity left considerable room for improvement. According to a study by the Economist Intelligence Unit (EIU), published in August 1995, Rover produced 14.3 vehicles per worker in 1994. Although that was well ahead of Volkswagen (12.5) it was way behind Ford (the European industry leader with 20.3 cars per worker), General Motors, Renault and Fiat. Moreover, in perhaps the key measure of sales per worker, the EIU study found that Rover lagged behind all but Fiat. By contrast, BMW lay second, behind only Mercedes but just ahead of GM.

It was becoming clearer by the day that the hands-off approach was not delivering the goods. BMW had no alternative but to step up the pace of change at Rover. To cope with both the competitive challenges and the transformation he wanted to engineer, Pischetsrieder believed that Rover needed gingering up. He was reported as saying that Rover's executive echelons lacked 'petrol-heads' – car enthusiasts with a real feel and zest for the business. Rover was about to get a fuel injection from Munich.

On 7 September BMW announced that Wolfgang Reitzle was taking over from Pischetsrieder as Rover chairman. The news caused a furore in the media, where the cultured Reitzle was immediately branded a hatchet man. 'There is going to be blood on the floor,' the *Daily Mail* quoted one Rover insider as saying. At BMW's annual British press dinner two months later, Pischetsrieder smiled: 'I have been to Rover many times recently, but I have not seen any blood.' He was not going to have to wait very long. The move also put a big question mark over the future of Towers, who was now seen as being subjected to Reitzle's direction.

Culture Clash

Reitzle was privately dismissive of Towers' abilities as chief executive and did little to hide his feelings. 'How can you get a car out of a Tower?' he once joked. 'The only thing they have in common is the letter "R".' Maybe the joke loses something in translation, but not in the sentiment behind it. Reitzle was unquestionably the most talented executive in BMW and Towers himself admitted he was the best 'product man in the business'. But the appointment was in one very important respect truly bizarre. Inside the Four Cylinder, it had always been Reitzle that had argued BMW should dispose of Rover cars, which he believed to be a dog whose day was long gone, and concentrate on Land Rover. Now he had been handed the responsibility for restoring a brand that he believed to be beyond redemption.

There was no way that Reitzle would continue to be a hands-off chairman in the Pischetsrieder fashion. Despite constant commuting his influence was soon being exerted. His natural inclination to focus on brand issues quickly came to the fore. No ideas were considered too radical. One of the many, for example, was to revive Triumph, a marque that had been unceremoniously dumped during the decline of British Leyland. The plan was to use Triumph to replace the existing Rover 200 and Rover 400 model ranges, due to be renewed around the turn of the century. The decision would have enabled BMW to move Rover further upmarket, focusing it on the Rover 600 and Rover 800 successor. It would also have helped BMW to relaunch Rover cars in America, where Triumph remained a well-recognized brand that had escaped the ignominy attached to Rover after the Sterling debacle of the late 1980s. Pischetsrieder and Reitzle were not entirely in discord over Rover cars. Both believed that Rover's existing product range, which extended from the Rover 100 (formerly the Metro) to the Rover 800, was far too wide.

They planned to replace the small Rovers with a new Mini, which would be marketed as a stand-alone brand, distinct from Rover. The Mini, codenamed R59 because the original had been launched in 1959, was planned to be a small car, which would be marketed worldwide through both Rover and BMW outlets and would replace the 100, thereby partly fulfilling BMW's aim of taking the Rover cars range upmarket. BMW–Rover aimed to sell 200,000 Minis a year worldwide, double the annual figure for sales of the 100 and the old Mini. Western Europe would be the main market for the car, but Asia and South America were also seen as potentially big sales areas, as was eastern Europe eventually. The family of cars was to be engineered and styled at BMW's Munich headquarters and in Britain.

A longer term issue was whether Longbridge would build the new Mini family. BMW considered making the Mini at Rover's Cowley plant in Oxford, but Pischetsrieder had always said the Mini should go to the Birmingham plant. 'The Mini is the British motor car, so where else on earth should it be built but at Longbridge?' he said. 'The factory is so much part of the Mini's identity. At Longbridge, you find people who have spent their entire working life helping to build the Mini.' Longbridge certainly needed Mini. In the mid-1990s, output there was running at only about two-thirds of its 450,000 cars a year capacity. The car was based on the floor-pan developed by BMW for its front-wheel drive City car prototype which ultimately failed to go into production.

For Pischetsrieder, the Mini was a pet project. He repeatedly insisted that the new Mini must break new ground in design and marketing. Pischetsrieder was, however, always cagey about when a new Mini could be launched, repeatedly suggesting that it might not come until the twenty-first century although privately BMW wanted to have it ready in 1999. However, urgency was injected into the Mini timetable by the need to reinvigorate Rover's small car range which was suffering by comparison with its rivals' mini and supermini segments. The new Mini range was to be a big boost for Rover dealers in Britain, who had been hit by Rover's shortcomings in the high volume, small car sector. At least three Mini variants were to be developed: a three-door hatchback, a five-door version and a Mini-van. The plan was to pitch the Mini upmarket of Volkswagen's new Beetle, which was aimed at the mass market.

Pischetsrieder was also considering merging the 200 and 400 mid-market models into a single range and that process would have been dramatized by the resurrection of Triumph. The last Triumph had been the Acclaim, a Honda car that was made at Cowley under an agreement between Sir Michael Edwardes, then BL chairman, and the Japanese. It was an undistinguished end to a famous career that earned Triumph a worldwide following. The Triumph debate inside BMW highlighted the problems of breathing life into the ailing Rover brand; and all of them basically consisted of ignoring the Rover name itself. Work had also started on Project Flagship, an executive saloon at the top of the range, which Pischetsrieder was thinking of calling Riley. Ever the Anglophile car buff, the BMW chief loved Rileys – even if scarcely anyone in Britain could remember what the Riley brand had stood for.

For Pischets rieder, the Mini was a pet project

Cultural incompatibility continued to dog BMW's attempts to revive Rover. The lid was eventually blown on the problem in an article in *Car Magazine* (September 1996), entitled 'The Marriage from Hell'. Widely believed to have been 'officially' leaked from within BMW, the article was replete with stories of Anglo-German tensions. The British were depicted as intransigent, arrogant and grasping. As one BMW manager put it, 'Rover's strengths seem to be the creation of unnecessary friction, a disappointing no-risk attitude, and an amazing display of egoism. There is a very obvious culture clash between our companies.'

An identical message emerged from the BBC documentary series *When Rover Met BMW*. The fact that the series was even allowed to be made is an indication of the loose management and exemplified the shortcomings of BMW's laissez-faire approach to Rover. It had been commissioned by Towers, never backward in the art of self-promotion, before the takeover. Instead of quietly transferring it to a distant backburner, as one would have expected BMW to do, the Germans allowed Towers to carry on. The result, it has to be said, was to give the television audience a rare insight into a struggling merger.

If one scene in *When Rover Met BMW* epitomized the depth of the problem, it was the moment when a poor catering lady laid on her best cheese and pineapple on cocktail sticks for Reitzle during a fleeting visit to Rover's Gaydon engineering centre. But the impatient Reitzle had a packed schedule and was running late when he arrived at Gaydon. The amiable Bernard Carey, head of corporate affairs, seemed blissfully unaware of Reizle's growing irritation as they sat in the traffic. We, the viewers, had a better view. Reitzle was very quietly seething. By the time the BMW engineering supremo was due to be tucking into the cheese and pineapple spread, he had decided he did not have time for the buffet lunch and swept out of Gaydon en route to another appointment. The sadness in the eyes of the lady as Reitzle disappeared was palpable and came straight from a Victoria Wood *Dinner Ladies* episode. Reitzle was oblivious to the sad tableau and the Rover people had never seen it coming. The lingering impression was of two organizations on completely different wavelengths. It was all too close to the truth.

Structure and Brand Realignment

Shortly after Reitzle's arrival, he scrapped the structure under which Rover had operated for five years and put a new emphasis on design and development by splitting engineering from manufacturing. Nick Stephenson of Rover was appointed to the new post of design and engineering director. His brief was to work closely to the BMW engineering maestros in

Munich, from where much of the basic design for Rover's future vehicles would be drawn. BMW's publicity stated that: 'Given Rover's own objectives of moving upmarket, the focus on product and technical excellence now needs to take a higher place in our strategic priorities'. Pischetsrieder and Reitzle believed the restructuring would allow BMW to increase the pace of change, enabling it to squeeze costs by handing component purchasing responsibility to Stephenson. It could also design in under-the-skin commonality between Rover cars, Land Rover vehicles and, eventually, BMW models. 'There will be much more cross-fertilisation between programmes,' said Pischetsrieder.

BMW was working to eliminate poor quality, which on models such as the Discovery led to high warranty costs. Pischetsrieder, who publicly described Land Rover quality as 'a scandal', added: 'It is quite clear that even the medium-term future for Rover cannot be selling fewer cars than BMW, when Rover has a much lower unit price. That is not going to work. Remember the whole purpose of building cars is to sell them for profit. That is why we have to globalize the Rover business and focus the Rover brand identity worldwide.'

Under Reitzle, responsibility for that task was eventually handed to Tom Purves, who in July 1996 was named Rover sales and marketing head. Steeped in the art of brand management, Purves had built a British market share of almost 3.5 per cent, more than double that of Mercedes. His record showed an impressive ability to sustain an exclusive image while achieving relatively high sales volumes, particularly for BMW's 3 series. 'It's a touch of pile 'em high and sell them quite expensively,' quipped one expert. Purves had come from BMW GB, the company's British marketing arm, where he had been managing director. Before that, he had been head of sales and marketing at Rolls-Royce Motors. Purves's style was in tune with his luxury and executive car background. The question was how well suited he was for the exacting task of hauling Rover's image out of the rational desert – the middle market no-man's land. Whatever the doubts, there was no question about the marketing road on which Rover was now set.

The ideas floated were clear indications that at last the message that things were not right was beginning to sink home. Unfortunately, while the symptoms were identified the disease was still largely undiagnosed. A later branding exercise was indicative of the problems facing Rover. The

Rover in-house video might well be viewed as a master class in under-whelming your audience. The Rover brand was to be encapsulated in the words *welcoming, effortless, craftsmanship, engineering, British style*. It is hard to imagine a less dynamic message. Would anyone in the Rover organization, let alone the paying customer, be galvanized into action by the lethargic and sanitized message delivered by the video. It was as if the Rover management expected a culture to be altered by a single, unfocused message. Brand is about perception, and the perception of the Rover brand was not about to alter overnight on the back of banalities like 'welcoming', 'craftsmanship' and 'British style'.

The fallacy of such a branding approach was reinforced by John Russell, Purves's predecessor. Rover had been running a series of ads with the tag line: 'Relax; it's a Rover.' While defending the 'relaxation' series of ads, which had been heavily criticized in the advertising media, Russell admitted the brand problem: 'If you have a strong brand even moderately good ads would be seen in a good light. But if the brand is struggling to express itself, and I don't say that Rover is, the ads tend to be judged in a more critical fashion' (*Marketing Week*, 4 October 1996). Russell was implicitly accepting the confusion surrounding the Rover brand. He added, in an attempt to rationalize the problem:

> 66 Rover is in a transitional period where its product has improved faster than the brand has developed. The Rover brand is lagging behind the technology but the next generation of products will give the opportunity for distinctive positioning as part of the BMW portfolio 99.

In reality the problem was that the brand perfectly reflected the range (or vice versa) which still had an undynamic image as an overpriced, middle-aged bank manager's car. 'Rovers are for people who wear hats and mow their lawn on Sundays,' said one entrepreneur dismissively. To make matters even worse the dynamic brands in the stable, such as MG and the Mini, were also languishing at that time, although they clearly had the potential to be revived. A few days after Russell's departure, Martin Runnacles, Purves's marketing expert at BMW GB, followed his boss to Rover. The transformation of the marketing domain completed the management restructure which had begun with Pischetsrieder's realization that BMW had to transplant into Rover BMW's intense engineering discipline and total marketing commitment.

Then Towers left – his departure memorably recorded by the BBC documentary cameras. His resignation, with a near-£500,000 golden handshake, reinforced the immersion of Rover into BMW. Pischetsrieder, commenting on Towers's departure, observed that, 'It was Caesar who said, "I would prefer to be the first in a village than the second in Rome".' He may have had a point about Towers but to refer to Rover in imperial terms was at best wishful thinking and at worst delusional. Rover was now costing BMW £600m a year in investment – at least 20 per cent more than it had anticipated and a reflection of the full extent of the under-investment which Rover had suffered for a decade. 'We have doubled the investment rate,' said Pischetsrieder. 'Rover would never have found those resources from its own cashflow.'

What was not so clear to Pischetsrieder at the time was that it had not been money well spent. In fact, the investment, plus an expected sales rise that year from 483,000 vehicles to about 540,000 worldwide, had failed to make much impact on Rover's results. Under BMW's accounting methods, the increased investment actually raised Rover's losses to £148m. Rover's own, less severe accounting system produced a £91m profit. Pischetsrieder explained that, on an international accounting standard, Rover was somewhere between a £10m loss and break-even, effectively a zero return. By contrast, BMW consistently aimed for between 6 per cent and 7 per cent pre-tax, and was close to that target. Pischetsrieder said, 'Whatever your accounting principles are, any successful car company has to achieve returns which are similar to BMW's. Otherwise, you won't be able to fund your long-term investment.' Rover's weak performance led Garel Rhys, Cardiff University Business School's professor of motor industry economics, to conclude:

> 66 Rover is still in the convalescent ward. There has been a lot of good news in terms of improving efficiency, getting rid of industrial-relations problems, and putting in Japanese-style working practices. But it still has to show itself in the bottom line. BMW realizes that if it isn't careful, it will find itself dragged down the way the strong and profitable Leyland Motors was by the British Motor Corporation after the formation of British Leyland 99 .

Despite the rough water, Pischetsrieder remained bullish. 'The last thing we are going to decide is what the cars are going to be called,' he said of Rover's future products. 'The core point of BMW's thinking is not about brand names, but about brand identity. The first thing we have to do is build a Rover brand identity and a solid presence in the market. You cannot do this in a hurry; you must be properly prepared because in this industry, you only have one shot. Will we get there? I have absolutely no doubt that we will.'

7

Evaluation

EVALUATING THE INITIAL PERIOD of BMW's ownership of Rover entails tapping into the emotional rationale of the major players. Essentially what characterizes that first period was the triumph of hope over experience. BMW, in the shape of Bernd Pischetsrieder, had so willingly bought into the 'volume equals independence' mantra that it was virtually forced to ignore reality in order to follow the chosen road. Pischetsrieder overlooked the need to root strategy in a deep understanding of current reality. He developed his strategy in spite of the reality, not in response to it. Ultimately, ignorance of two huge chunks of reality proved disastrous. The first was the 'brand' reality of which much has already been mentioned. However, it is worth adding that Pischetsrieder was as aware of brand significance as anyone; he just misjudged the gravity of Rover's brand sickness. The second ignorance was of 'cultural' reality. What is clear is that Pischetsrieder was too concerned about perceived British sensitivities and also too convinced of his own ability to reconcile those sensitivities.

Pischetsrieder was wrong to choose 'persuasion' over 'purging' with the senior management. Britain had survived Thatcherism and its workforce understood that managers pay the price for underperformance, the high attrition rate in football being their convenient analogy. They were not concerned with attrition among management, only among workers. They actually saw the arrival of BMW as an affirmation of their value as a workforce and generally welcomed the situation. Pischetsrieder himself once observed that 'deep in the culture of Rover is the notion that whoever Big Brother is, he will care for us'. He was precisely right; the workforce want what's best for them, irrespective of who provides it.

The 'political' issues which so concerned Pischetsrieder were also largely irrelevant. Again, self-interests (votes) were mostly in safe Labour strongholds and the Conservatives had previously approved Jaguar's sale without any lasting impact on their image. None of the cultural sensitivities warranted threatening the bottom line by continuing with a weak management team. Pischetsrieder was, therefore, equally wrong in choosing a hands-off management style. Leaving a disaffected Towers in place was bad enough, but failing to exercise a controlling influence over a potentially disruptive influence was tantamount to negligence. Getting rid of Towers early in the process may have caused some short-term difficulties, but it might also have enabled BMW to retain some of the others who subsequently had to go. Formally using Towers as only the Honda relationship man would have been much more sensible.

It is always easier to soften a hard approach than to harden a soft approach

Eventually, Pischetsrieder was forced to purge. It would have been more effective had it been done earlier. It is always easier to soften a hard approach than to harden a soft approach. The arrival of Reitzle to play the hard man in implementing a strategy for which he had little time was also an unhelpful decision on Pischetsrieder's part. Reitzle's distaste for the role was evident and he moved aside as soon as an opportunity presented itself, which was an indication of his level of commitment.

It is clear that Pischetsrieder failed to engage in any genuine investigation of the culture into which he would be immersed and as such he made small but hugely significant mistakes. The June 2000 edition of the *Harvard Business Review* featured a discussion between several well-known managers concerning post-merger issues. Most agreed that success depends upon fostering a culture of respect and involvement. Dennis Kozlowski, chief executive of Tyco International, the acquisitive manufacturing and services group, argued that it is 'almost impossible to build such a culture when you do hostile acquisitions'.

Rover was not a hostile acquisition – at the time. But because BMW did not integrate Rover with its existing operations, the two sides of the group continued to co-exist: first uneasily, then with increasing resentment on the BMW brand side as Rover's losses continued. The problem was compounded when Rover engineering and other functions were belatedly made subject to Munich. As Rover insiders saw it, instead of reporting independently to a BMW group committee, Rover had to report through the people running the BMW brand, who took decisions in their own interest, often to Rover's detriment.

For 18 months, instead of suppressing expectations BMW fed them. Doing so merely increased the likelihood of failure. Reitzle's arrival provided the opportunity to take stock and change course. When he returned to Munich, Pischetsrieder probably had one last chance to get the huge Rover recovery task back on track. That chance was lost, and with it went Rover's last meaningful hope of survival.

PART THREE

Sir Walter's Rally

CHAPTER 8

Overlapping Strategy

D URING THE SIX-MONTH HIATUS after John Towers' departure in April 1996, Pischetsrieder searched for a British replacement to work in tandem with Wolfgang Reitzle. Asked why he wanted a British chief executive, he replied that he still believed a British chief executive would be best qualified to reinforce the Britishness of Rover's new model range – despite the increasing evidence that Rover needed more managerial influence from BMW rather than less. Initially BMW sounded out Ian Gibson, the former Ford manager who had led Nissan's Sunderland factory to productivity pre-eminence in the European industry. But Gibson was not interested in moving from the job he had effectively created to the potentially disastrous environment of the West Midlands.

In the end, Pischetsrieder found what seemed a perfect solution: he appointed Walter Hasselkus, an Anglophile whose affection for the British dated from his time in the early 1980s as head of BMW GB. The 54-year-old Hasselkus's courteous manner and his English experience had earned him the nickname 'Sir Walter' at the Four Cylinder. But there was mettle behind the gentility: he had earned his spurs by turning round BMW's Berlin-based, loss-making motorbike arm. The challenge facing Hasselkus at Rover, however, was of an altogether different magnitude. For one thing, the industrial environment was forbidding. The European motor industry was in a period of ultra-competition. As Reitzle later pointed out, the improvement in the quality of all cars meant that product differentiation was increasingly narrowing while price competition was always intensifying.

The productivity gains being made across Europe were fuelling overcapacity by increasing the ability of car firms to make more cars than the market wanted. Western Europe could build 20m cars a year, but sold only 13m. All this added up to an intensity of competition last seen in the 1920s. It was great news for consumers, of course, unless they also happened to be car workers. Jac Nasser, then Ford's global automotive chief, said: 'All of us will start to look at opportunities to get our costs in line with revenue. The Japanese and Koreans are taking more market share. These events are not unconnected.'

At the same time, Japanese output, particularly from the British trans-plants of Nissan, Honda and Toyota, was soaring. Ian Robertson of the Economist Intelligence Unit believed that the 'Japanese production in Europe would climb from 715,000 vehicles last year to 1.2m in 2000'.

Western Europe could build 20m cars a year, but sold only 13m. All this added up to an intensity of competition last seen in the 1920s

Alex Trotman, Ford's chairman, said the previous year western Europe had the capacity to build 20m vehicles a year with little prospect of improving on the 12.8m sales of 1996. Keith Hayes, Goldman Sachs' European motor industry analyst, said, 'If overall productivity has been rising at about 5 per cent a year, utilization rates could be struggling to remain much above 70 per cent even at the peak of the cycle.' The result of this oversupply was becoming evident in the marketplace: price competition was cutthroat, and the cost of sales was spiralling. Ford of Europe had racked up losses of almost £188m. Fiat's European car arm was also in, or close to, the red. Peugeot was still profitable but even those profits were slumping. And at the same time as they were being squeezed by price pressures, the Europeans were also having to satisfy increasingly demanding consumers. 'There have been dramatic changes in the market and in customer behaviour over the last several years,' said Nasser at the time. Consumers wanted new products and a greater variety – and all at acceptable prices. They were also buying smaller cars. As Nasser pointed out, 'The European consumer has downsized by almost one and a half categories.'

The result of those trends was to create huge demands on the carmakers' resources, particularly as profit margins on smaller products were wafer thin. Previously they could have partly compensated by boosting sales through exports, but that safety valve was closing because countries in Asia and Latin America were demanding local manufacture. Goldman's Hayes said: 'If the Europeans don't bite the bullet [and close factories], they will be condemned to years of what will be, to put it politely, subdued profitability.'

It was becoming obvious that the weaker players or plants would be squeezed. And it meant that, once significant ground was lost, it would be increasingly difficult to recover. This was not like the 1960s, when BMW had laid the foundations for its amazing resurgence. Now, because of the difficulty of making a decent return on investment, it would be ever more difficult to justify the spending necessary to turn a marginal marque or factory into a mainstream contender. For BMW, which had acquired Rover precisely in order to increase capacity, the dilemma was acute. It also meant Hasselkus and his new team, with Purves and Runnacles leading the sales and marketing side, had little margin for error and less time than they would have liked in which to get Rover on the right road. If anything, time was even more important than the money BMW was pouring into Rover. More than 15 months on from the takeover, BMW had still not fixed its product or plant strategy for Rover. The only firm decisions had been the 600 replacement and the development of Freelander as a 100 per cent Rover project.

Even the planned Mini, to which Pischetsrieder had been committed from day one of the takeover, was delayed. The original objective had been to have it in the showrooms in 1999, 40 years on from the launch of Issigonis's Mini. But the project was bounced from Munich to Gaydon and back again as BMW and Rover executives debated its design and how it should be marketed. The Mini was at the crux of two key choices that BMW had to make. With Rover cars, Pischetsrieder and Reitzle had to decide whether to proceed with the Mini project or to replace the Rover 200 and 400, the last two Honda-derived cars, first. With Land Rover, they had the option of developing a new Range Rover or a completely new Discovery.

The decision on the cars side could not be separated from the plant strategy. From the outset, there had been a running debate inside BMW and Rover about whether they should close Cowley and concentrate everything at Longbridge; do the reverse, and concentrate at Cowley; or keep both plants going. Each alternative had disadvantages: Longbridge needed massive investment, while Cowley, which had been partly redeveloped under BAe, was a more compact site and would be less expensive to modernize.

However, Cowley did not have Longbridge's capacity to build a full range of Rover cars. The decision hinged on Pischetsrieder's commitment to the 'overlap' product strategy – developing a full line of Rover cars that would, at the larger end, overlap with BMW models. He was fiercely opposed by Reitzle, who argued that Rover should be developed as a comple- mentary brand, focusing on Land Rover and cars smaller than or distinct from the BMW 'compact' 3- series. That essentially meant Mini, although it could also have encompassed MG. It would have entailed huge redundancies at Rover, through the closure of Longbridge, and among its thousands of component and service suppliers, and severe cuts in the dealer network.

Short-term opportunities should not take priority over long-term opportunities

Not only had this internal debate remained unresolved before the Rover acquisition, it ran on, intense but hidden from public view, for more than a year thereafter. Pischetsrieder alluded to it in his statement in BMW's 1995 annual report, published in April 1996.

> Short-term opportunism should not take priority over long-term opportunities. It should be disregarded if it is incompatible with the established identity of the company and its marques. That is why decisions which are right and necessary in the medium to long-term must be taken, even if they look risky or wrong in the short term.

Deliberately or not, the statement evoked the philosophy that von Kuenheim had articulated years earlier, when he said: 'Success in industry doesn't just emerge through short-term activities. It results from long-term efforts and insights. You have to have visions of the future. If these are right, then you might see the benefits after five or ten years.'

Pischetsrieder won the supervisory board's endorsement for his overlap strategy, later thanking his colleagues – according to *Manager* magazine – for their 'considerable personal backing'. A few months later, shortly after

Hasselkus's appointment, Pischetsrieder lifted a corner of the curtain that had concealed the argument when he addressed BMW's annual November top management conference at the Vier Jahreszeiten in Munich, attended by BMW and Rover executives.

'You know that this overlapping of product ranges has been discussed for a long time and in detail,' Pischetsrieder told his audience. 'A complementary product programme would have meant in the car area of the group only vehicles below the BMW Compact (small saloon) and Land Rover vehicles – that is, giving up the previous Rover car models,' he said. 'This strategy was finally rejected, although there would have been good grounds for it,' said Pischetsrieder. 'The way we have opted for is indeed more difficult, but just as rich in opportunity.' The overlap strategy meant, he said, that 'as well as the tailor-made Italian suit for which BMW might stand, there would also be the comfortable and nevertheless elegantly tailored suit from the London workshop for which Rover cars might stand.'

The overlap vision was the basis for the Rover takeover, and therefore consistent with the strategy that underpinned it. But the product and plant plan that emerged stored up problems which could threaten achievement of the strategy. The outcome of the internal debate was a dangerous compromise. BMW committed to Pischetsrieder's overlap strategy, but in key segments it made the 'complementary' models its product priorities.

As soon as he got his feet under the table at Rover, Hasselkus announced that the Mini would be produced at Longbridge (it was to be launched in 2001, although he did not say so specifically). It would be an upmarket car with a price tag to match. Analysts took that to mean it would be priced at around £12,000, against the old Mini's then price of £9000. A replacement for the 200 and 400 would come later. At Land Rover, rather than concentrate on Discovery, BMW would develop a completely new Range Rover, again for launch in 2001. But because of the quality problems and design faults of the current Discovery, an improved version would be developed based on the existing design but extensively re-engineered. This interim solution was codenamed Tempest, which turned out to be very appropriate since the project ran into costly turbulence.

For the BMW group, the advantages of this strategy were clear: it would recreate two premium models – Mini, which was to be separated from Rover, and Range Rover, which was to be repositioned as the Rolls-Royce of off-roaders with a price tag to match – close to £100,000. Range Rover was, above all, Reitzle's vision. Rover had only launched a new Range Rover the previous autumn, but on his first visit to Land Rover after the BMW acquisition, Reitzle had climbed into the new vehicle, donned an aircraft eye mask and spent five minutes touching every inch of the cabin. He then got out and wrote a list of 70 features that he believed should be changed. However, the 'Range Rover first' strategy was not just Reitzle's, it was also dictated by BMW's own brand priorities.

Pischetsrieder told the management summit that there had to be 'clear alternatives' in the same vehicle categories. 'Therefore, as well as the traditional Land Rover with its all-terrain capability, there should also be a car which has the essential characteristics of an all-terrain vehicle.' This was the rationale for BMW's X5, whose economics could only be justified because it shared a floor-pan with the new Range Rover. The problem was that this strategy left Discovery out on a limb: its sales ran down and, when it belatedly emerged, Tempest never regained the 1995 sales peak of the original model.

The product compromise was compounded by the decision to retain both Cowley and Longbridge. For Pischetsrieder and von Kuenheim, the alternative – axing Cowley with the loss of thousands of jobs – was unpalatable. The result should have been at least equally unpalatable. Rover retained huge capacity that would cost billions of pounds to modernize and take years, at best, to fill: the time–money paradox was again at work. How BMW planned to fill those production lines had also become clear. By 2002, Rover was to produce 470,000 Rover-badged cars, 200,000 Minis, 30,000 MGs and 200,000 Land Rovers: 900,000 vehicles in all. At Rover cars and Land Rover, the die was now cast. Within two months of Hasselkus's arrival, Reitzle relinquished the Rover chairmanship and focused entirely on his work in Munich. There, he had a large group of supporters who harboured deep misgivings about the overlap strategy – and had done so from the very start of the Rover expedition.

Hasselkus, who now added the chairman's title to his portfolio, had no doubt about his objective: 'I'm determined and completely dedicated to making Rover a profitable, commercially successful, fully fledged company, which is respected as a player in car-business terms worldwide,' he said. He was also confident of attaining those goals. 'When I retire, with luck a good few years down the line,' he said in January 1997, 'I hope we are flush with money so that they can throw a proper farewell.'

While bemoaning the fact that it was still almost impossible to find a source of good German wines in England, Hasselkus believed his knowledge of the British could help to bridge the cultural divide between the Rover and BMW managers and engineers. There was, for instance, 'a language issue. When a British manager says, "there could be a slight problem here", a German thinks that is the situation. Whereas I know it means we have a real problem,' he said with a smile. Rover certainly had a *slight* problem. It was heading for a hefty full-year loss which emerged at £103m for 1996, only slightly down on the previous year's £128m. Hasselkus pointed out that BMW's accounting treatment of currency translation and depreciation added £200m to Rover's loss. Rover also passed two milestones: sales exceeded 500,000, the highest level since 1988, and for the first time the group sold more vehicles overseas than in Britain. Things appeared to be turning.

However, even if the severe accounting standards were discounted, the fact remained that Rover cars was deep in loss while Land Rover was making good money. According to *Manager* magazine, Land Rover made about almost £9000 per vehicle, or £88m in the year, and we now know that Rover was *losing* money on every car. Hasselkus instituted an austerity regime that included the requirement that all office lights be switched off after they were vacated at 5 pm. Optional marketing expenses were also cut to the bone as Hasselkus set about husbanding resources for the expansion drive. The workforce, which had ballooned to more than 40,000 in the two years since the takeover, was trimmed to 39,400. Hasselkus also ended the complete division that had existed between Munich and the West Midlands. He merged engineering and set about rationalizing procurement. BMW announced that within four months all parts purchasing for Rover would be handled from Munich. By buying parts together in bigger volume, BMW and Rover planned to cut the cost of some parts by 10 per cent or more.

Tony Woodley, the Transport & General Workers Union's chief motor industry negotiator, observed: 'The honeymoon is over. Rover is now very much under the control of BMW' (*Business Week*, 24 March 1997). Pischets-rieder was still insisting that the acquisition would be cost effective. His argument was that even in the worst case – four years of losses plus the purchase price – Rover would only have cost BMW £1.3bn. 'For this today you could not get either a 3-Series range or a comparable competitive offer on the market,' he told *Manager* magazine. But the calculations were wildly optimistic and took no account of the billions of pounds BMW was having to pump into Rover to remedy decades of under-investment.

Outside Help?

Behind the scenes, however, even Pischetsrieder was beginning to wonder whether Rover would eventually need some outside help, in the form of a big brother, to pull through the promised renaissance. Reitzle had a ready-made contact. The previous summer, while he was still Rover chairman, he had hosted a visit to Longbridge by Bob Lutz, president of Chrysler, America's third largest carmaker. The flamboyant Lutz was not only second in command to Chrysler's chairman, Bob Eaton, he had previously worked at BMW as sales director, alongside Reitzle. Chrysler and BMW were a good match. Unlike General Motors and Ford, Chrysler had little overseas presence and lacked financial muscle. It could therefore use a European partner. It had recently held extensive discussions with Mercedes-Benz about a possible joint venture, codenamed Q-Star, but these had come to nothing. And the truth was that Lutz preferred BMW: 'Mercedes was always after some big, global solution,' he told Bill Vlasic and Bradle Stertz, authors of *Taken For A Ride*. 'There is more of a kinship with BMW. We're both number three. They're more like us. Neither of us can be like the other guys. To survive, we both have to be unconventional, different, fast.'

The Chrysler–BMW talks soon bore fruit. Early in 1997, they announced a $500m joint venture to make 400,000 small car engines a year in Brazil. BMW intended to put the engines in the new Mini. News of the alliance spooked Mercedes, where executives saw it as the first step on the road to a mega-merger. While avoiding merger speculation, Pischetsrieder confirmed that he saw Chrysler as BMW's first-choice ally: 'If we find other opportunities for a joint venture, Chrysler would be our partner, whether in a vehicle, steering system or anything else,' he told *Automotive News* Europe. Lutz was singing the same tune: 'If we were to envisage a more important co-operative project, it would be with BMW,' he said.

What that more important project could be was obvious: Chrysler could help Rover re-enter the American market, by providing distribution or manufacturing capacity, while some of Rover's spare capacity could be devoted to providing Chrysler with a European manufacturing presence in cars (it already had a joint venture with Steyr in Austria to make Jeeps). Further, the two companies could develop a new model which on the BMW side could become the replacement for the Rover 200 and 400. Chrysler would make it for both companies in the USA; Rover could badge the product for Chrysler in Europe.

Schrempp cut off BMW's most natural escape route from the Rover imbroglio – a fact of which he was no doubt well aware

According to *Automotive News*, the industry publication, Chrysler might also have supplied 1.8 litre and 2.0 litre engines for the model – although that would have involved a rethink on BMW's planned second phase of its £450m Hams Hall engine plant for which the government had agreed to provide £45m in aid. All 1.4 litre and 1.6 litre engines for the medium-sized car could have been built at the Brazil factory. A deal with Chrysler would have solved many of the problems that eventually killed BMW's great Rover project. Instead, the possibility, distinct as it was, became one of the industry's might have beens. The following year, Jurgen Schrempp, chairman of DaimlerChrysler which had by then taken full control of Mercedes, won Eaton's agreement to the mega-merger that is described in *Taken For A Ride*. In the process, Schrempp cut off BMW's most natural escape route from the Rover imbroglio – a fact of which he was no doubt well aware.

Working Practices

While the Chrysler contacts continued, Hasselkus ploughed his own furrow in an attempt to put Rover on solid foundations for growth. One of his biggest challenges concerned the unions. Under the umbrella of a change programme called The Way Ahead, Hasselkus also initiated talks with the Rover unions over a new flexible working package. In return for guaranteeing the jobs of Rover's employees, Hasselkus wanted cuts in operating costs and higher productivity. He wanted an agreement that would allow working hours to be varied according to demand and to end shift bonuses. Such reforms would clear the way for production of the new Mini at Longbridge. The Birmingham plant was to be revamped later in 1997, when production of the Rover 100 would be phased out.

In order to avoid big job losses, Hasselkus also wanted to transfer workers from Longbridge to Land Rover at Solihull until the Mini and a new engine plant, which BMW was planning at Hams Hall near Birmingham, came on stream. Hasselkus wanted to scrap the time-honoured system of a fixed basic wage with additional overtime and bonus payments. In its place he wanted workers to operate within a framework of total annual hours. Pay rates and holidays would increase, but the working day would be longer. While BMW operated its Bavarian plants on this basis, the concept was traditionally unacceptable to the British working culture.

Warwick University's Bhattacharyya believed a revolution in factory operation was taking place. 'The companies are trying to get absolute flexibility in the utilization of their resources,' he said. 'If you are going to invest hundreds of millions of pounds, you want total output. We are moving towards a form of continuous production, like the chemical industry. The car industry has never worked this way in most of west Europe.' In a bid to contain spiralling development costs, companies would increasingly be driven to pool their resources. According to Bhattacharyya, 'The days of independent manufacturing are numbered.'

Hasselkus's proposals required the co-operation or at least non-resistance of the workforce. Under Towers, Rover had agreed a 'new deal' with the unions in 1991. That guaranteed the jobs of the 39,000 workers for life in exchange for a greater degree of flexibility. What BMW wanted was effectively to buy out that guarantee. Hasselkus planned to streamline Rover's workforce – by voluntary redundancy – and to transform productivity. If the deal was agreed, several thousand jobs would disappear. Woodley, chairman of the unions' joint negotiating committee, signalled a willingness to discuss changes to the New Deal arrangements. However, as he told *Business Week*, the American magazine, 'We are not going to keel over and have our bellies tickled.'

The problem for Hasselkus was that negotiations would have to have taken place alongside talks about that year's pay settlement. If BMW pushed to buy out the agreement, then the unions would have sought generous purchase terms and a pledge that there would be no compulsory redundancies. BMW's urgent need to increase efficiency, therefore, simultaneously strengthened and weakened the unions' negotiating position. Ironically, only a month or so earlier Woodley had joined forces with Rover in a bid to save more than 1000 jobs under threat at Rover's Longbridge plant in Birmingham where the Mini, Rover 200, Rover 400 and most of Rover's engines were made.

In a letter headed 'Mobility – Why the need?', Woodley and Harry Dunlevy, Rover's personnel director, wrote urging 'associates' (as Rover called its workers) to agree one of the biggest transfers of staff in recent British industrial history. According to the letter, more than 1000 extra workers would be needed in 1997 and 1998 at Land Rover's Solihull plant, where a new small Land Rover was to increase the product range. But, said the letter, 'due to reducing volumes and productivity improvements in small and medium cars, Longbridge will need to reduce its headcount by over 1,000 in 1997 and beyond'. The reason for the cut was that Rover was about to axe production of the Rover 100. Longbridge's production was planned to pick up in 2001 with the new Mini, but Hasselkus wanted union agreement to Japanese-style working flexibility before finally committing to build Minis at Longbridge.

Despite the New Deal there had, in reality, always been some voluntary redundancies of older workers at Cowley. Given that fact, and the scope for efficiency improvements at Longbridge, the new working practices were likely to be agreed by the union which was in a difficult position with production at 32 cars per body and assembly worker, well below the European average. The working practices issue was to rumble on throughout the BMW–Rover saga and Hasselkus had only just encountered its first manifestation. The initial euphoria of the workforce at BMW's arrival had given way to a certain concern. Woodley's comment about keeling over and having their 'bellies tickled' indicated a level of suspicion between management and worker. This was an impediment Hasselkus could well have done without. In fact, the situation was clearly one that could not be left to fester and the pay negotiations were brought forward from November.

According to David Bower, Rover's personnel director, the change in date was the direct result of the revival that Hasselkus was trying to engineer. What Bower referred to as a series of major decisions were expected over the ensuing months. Bower recognized that: 'Job insecurity is a major issue and this [deal] offers us a significant period of stability for the workforce and real certainty on the part of the company about expectations and risks to payroll.' The deal he referred to provided for a general increase of 3.5 per cent in the first year from 1 November 1997. In years two and three, the rise would be inflation plus half a per cent or 3.5 per cent, whichever was the higher. For 'associates' who had been with the company for at least 12 months, a further 1 per cent would be paid the next year. And in a further fillip for trade unions, a German-style holiday bonus was to be introduced to make up for the loss of profit-related pay. Bower further explained that the planned green-field engine plant at Hams Hall would be Rover's template for the new working practices. 'We have been engaged in a two-year exercise with trade unions in benchmarking the best working practices in car-building around the world,' he said. 'All sites are going to be influenced by the working practices set in place at Hams Hall.'

CHAPTER **9** **Rapids Ahead!**

O N 4 JULY 1997 union leaders agreed a three-year pay deal that guaranteed jobs and investment at Rover. An immediate consequence was a pledge by Pischetsrieder and his fellow directors to build the new Mini at Longbridge and to launch it in late 1999, with the car going on sale in 2000 and building up to annual production of 150,000. The agreed package was worth a 6.5 per cent rise in year one, with 4.8 per cent rises in each of the following years. 'Part of our claim was to get guarantees on jobs, wages and plant security, and we have secured this,' Woodley said. Rover reaffirmed its 'new deal' agreement under which workers are offered jobs in other areas to avoid redundancy. It appeared that Hasselkus had successfully negotiated the obstacles to the first part of his revival plans. It remained to be seen whether he could navigate the rapids he was unknowingly approaching.

A section of those rapids was represented by Land Rover which posed a different problem. Pischetsrieder had already attempted to shock the staff there into awareness of its shortcomings. In a carefully calculated public outburst, he castigated Land Rover quality as 'a scandal'. Just as Land Rover had kept itself largely immune from the Honda influence on Rover cars, so the Solihull operation was proving increasingly resistant to BMW intervention. Land Rover workers themselves were considered by BMW people as the most intransigent of all their new British colleagues. One German engineer told *Car* magazine: 'From the beginning, the Land Rover guys were ten times worse than the passenger car people. Because they were successful and profitable, they were not prepared to listen. Build quality is appalling, active safety standards vary enormously, and the willingness to acknowledge and fix faults was, early on, absolutely zero,' the engineer said.

In America, Land Rover was placed forty-seventh out of 52 vehicles in the light truck segment of the early 1997 survey by JD Power, which measures faults per vehicle during the first three months of ownership and is regarded as the most authoritative independent gauge of quality in the car industry. Rover had skidded from thirty-eighth position in the previous year's survey when it had purportedly been at its worst. A Rover spokesman said at the time that Range Rover's decline was due to a product recall that astonishingly logged a problem on every Range Rover sold during the survey period. Admittedly there was a variety of reasons for the decline because, as a spokesman pointed out, the JD Power survey showed that Land Rover quality was indeed improving. 'The survey shows that Land Rover is the most improved brand in the list,' the spokesman said. 'But because the whole market has raised quality, we have not caught up by much.' One sign that Land Rover was moving in the right direction was that Discovery, its biggest selling model in America, rose from thirty-third to thirty-first place in the light truck sector.

The problem for Rover was that *absolute* improvement in a highly competitive market is largely irrelevant. What is essential in such a market is *relative* improvement

The problem for Rover was that *absolute* improvement in a highly competitive market is largely irrelevant. What is essential in such a market is *relative* improvement. Relatively, Land Rover was struggling. The competition was intensifying in the four-wheel drive market, not abating. Thanks to Discovery, Land Rover had enjoyed two years of soaring sales in America, but in 1997 sales were down on the corresponding 1996 period. Project Tempest was designed by Reitzle to restore the sales growth. However, while the revamped Discovery was a huge improvement in terms of quality and reliability, that improvement was achieved at a price. The re-engineered Discovery proved so heavy that Land Rover had to reinforce the floor of the Solihull paint shop to accommodate it. Such necessities meant Tempest impacted Land Rover profits. Although it temporarily raised sales when it was launched in 1998, the decline in Discovery demand soon resumed.

Relief for Land Rover came early in September 1997, when the Frankfurt Motor Show, Europe's top car jamboree, saw the debut of Freelander, the small Land Rover, and a version of the new Mini, destined for launch in 2001. With Range Rover and Discovery increasingly facing rival, lower priced products, the small four-by-four could not have been more timely. Rover was soon hiring workers to meet Freelander demand that was expected to reach 60,000 in a full year, expanding Land Rover's output by almost 50 per cent. Hasselkus felt that 'Freelander comes at the right time and is very good for Solihull and the dealer network'.

Two weeks after Frankfurt, Hasselkus unveiled a new corporate identity designed to distance the Rover group from its constituent brands and project a softer, more leisurely corporate image. Rover's advertising had already been adjusted along these lines by Purves. In place of the 'Above all, it's a Rover' slogan that had tried – and generally failed – to establish a distinctive niche for the marque, Purves was committed to trying to revive Rover's old upmarket reputation for solidity and comfort. 'The short and medium-term problems have to be overcome, and the BMW board and shareholders need to show some patience. But the general direction is the right one and it will pay off,' said Hasselkus. BMW had, he said, also finally discarded BMW's original hands-off attitude, which did nobody, least of all Rover, any favours. 'We don't talk any more about BMW and Rover; it's one company. The teams are working so closely together.'

Rhetorically that may have been true, but there was little evidence to support such an assertion. John Lawson, Salomon Brothers' European motor industry analyst, said at the time that the message was getting through: 'BMW's determination to see this turnaround through is infusing Rover. People feel they have been put on a course that nobody will be blown off. It is a more costly course than when BMW first embarked on it, but they haven't flinched and I don't believe they will.' In reality it was Lawson who had been infused with the tone of BMW's rhetoric; few at Rover felt the same way.

The level of investment could not be faulted. The Germans had ploughed in £600m in 1997, 20 per cent more than the previous year and more than double Rover's net cash flow. BMW was also transferring engineering and manufacturing expertise, primarily in the shape of a new quality director from Munich, Hans-Peter Lange, who was to report directly to Hasselkus and whose job was to install BMW's quality control and process methods at Rover plants. However, in order to placate any Rover sensitivities, BMW managers did not take over entirely. A Rover executive was earmarked to succeed Alan Curtis, manufacturing director, who had been seconded earlier that month to an important role with Rover's long-time adviser, Kumar Bhattacharyya. But the departure of Curtis, who had played a key role under George Simpson in setting up the BMW deal, in a way symbolized how the sense of a new dawn that had attended the BMW takeover had faded.

The BMW marketing influence was also becoming more apparent. Responding to criticism that the Rover 400 was an Escort-sized saloon at a Mondeo price, Hasselkus and Purves enhanced its specifications. They also launched a determined effort to boost the quality of Rover's British revenues, ceding low margin fleet sales – 30 per cent down in the first eight months of 1997 – but raising retail sales by 19 per cent. The dealer network was streamlined from 500 outlets to 350, so throughput per dealer in August was up almost 45 per cent. The changes made the franchise 'healthier and much more attractive', said Hasselkus. Worldwide, Rover and Land Rover sales in the first eight months of 1997 were slightly up on the corresponding period of the previous year. The star turn was the Rover 200, which had lifted sales sharply in Britain while surging ahead in Italy with a five-fold rise. Hasselkus argued that the Italian success was due more to competitiveness than to the Italian government's programme of incentives to buy new cars – a moot point.

While Hasselkus concentrated on Rover, Pischetsrieder's attention was temporarily elsewhere. There was one further acquisition to be made in order to fill the elite niche portfolio BMW envisaged. Pischetsrieder made little secret of his ambition. On a mild October evening in 1995, at BMW's annual British press dinner, he had picked up his table napkin and pulled out a pen. On the napkin, Pischetsrieder sketched a diagram showing how BMW had been reorganized since the Rover deal. 'We are now a holding company for a series of premium brands,' he said. 'We have Mini, MG, Rover, Land Rover, BMW. And, at the high end of the market, we have a gap. It would be filled very nicely by Rolls-Royce.'

In 1992, when von Kuenheim was still executive chairman, BMW had held protracted talks with Vickers, owner of Rolls-Royce and Bentley, about buying the business. A deal had been constructed in which BMW would take 60 per cent of Rolls-Royce, with Rolls-Royce plc, the aero-engine group that owned the marque, and Vickers each retaining 20 per cent. Eventually, BMW would move to full ownership. But faced with the challenge of building Spartanburg and worried by the prospect of having to axe thousands of jobs at Rolls' over-manned Crewe factory, BMW pulled out of the deal at the eleventh hour.

Then, in early 1998, Vickers – facing the threat of a takeover bid from the engineering company Mayflower – put Rolls-Royce back on the market. This time, BMW was totally committed to buy the company. Rolls had been streamlined and had considerable potential for expansion. Pischetsrieder tabled an initial offer of £250m. The offer was rejected, but BMW held what seemed to be two aces: first, it had already contracted to supply engines to the next generation of Rolls and Bentley four-door models, called respectively the Silver Seraph and the Arnage. Second, BMW was well supported by Rolls-Royce plc, with which von Kuenheim had forged a joint venture in small aero-engines in the early 1990s. At that time, BMW had taken a 3 per cent stake in Rolls-Royce and von Kuenheim and Sir Ralph Robins, Rolls' chairman, had considered an eventual merger of the two groups to create a European engineering powerhouse. The merger never came off, but Robins and von Kuenheim retained close links. Under a 1973 agreement, Rolls-Royce plc had the power to veto the sale of the Rolls-Royce name and trade-marks (the famous grille and Flying Lady emblem) to a foreign owner.

Despite its inside track, BMW had competition for Rolls. Schrempp had looked closely at the business, but his offer to agree a pre-emptive deal with Vickers was rejected by Sir Colin Chandler, Vickers' chairman. Daimler pulled out, unwilling to participate in an auction. Ferdinand Piech of Volkswagen, however, had no such qualms. Advised by the American investment bank Morgan Stanley, Piech set about breaking through the BMW–Rolls-Royce plc combination.

The attempted purchase of Rolls-Royce was another indication that BMW was pushing on with its package of niche products policy, irrespective of other considerations. Rolls Royce, for example, was a company whose products had become outdated to the point of embarrassing vulgarity. Even the new Silver Seraph was described by the *Economist* (4 April 1998) as 'Kitsch Britannia rather than Cool Britannia'. Pischetrieder was convinced that the problems related to RR were far less than the opportunities. In his view the only constraint on the luxury segment was demand and not supply. Improving supply would create its own demand.

In April, it looked as if Pischetrieder had won his prize with what appeared to be a winning bid of £340m. However, Piech would not lie down – a development that Pischetsrieder had anticipated early in the bid, when he confided to one commentator that Piech might bid £100m more than BMW. That is precisely what happened. At the eleventh hour, Piech produced a bid worth £430m. Chandler promptly declared VW the winner. Robins was furious, but Rolls-Royce plc's chances of blocking the takeover looked slim, despite the 1973 agreement which was in any case under investigation by the European Commission.

Pischetsrieder was ready to leave the field to Piech, but von Kuenheim would not give up. The old maestro, in a last hurrah for the company which he had served with such distinction for so long, warned Piech that BMW would not continue to supply Rolls and Bentley with engines unless VW ceded Rolls-Royce to BMW. This was the card that BMW had persuaded Honda not to play after the Rover takeover. BMW's notice period was one year, and Piech concluded that VW could not develop an engine in time to replace the BMW unit. He surrendered, and ownership of Rolls-Royce and Bentley was split. Piech kept Bentley – in which he was more interested than Rolls – the Crewe factory and Rolls for only four years. On 1 January 2003, ownership of the marque would pass to BMW. The truth is that Piech might have been able to tough it out. So unpopular with Silver Seraph customers did the BMW engine prove – it simply lacked the torque necessary to move such a heavy car – that it had to be replaced with the original Rolls-Royce V6 engine.

Pischetsrieder was delighted by the outcome of the Rolls battle:

> 66 You can either use this brand as an icon, sticking to a very high price and a very limited volume, or you can exploit it, with the risk that in 20 years it won't be worth any more than it is today. That is what VW is going to do [with Bentley]. They will go for 10,000-unit volume. Our strategy is to keep Rolls as an icon and limit sales to 1,000 units a year. What we can do is to exploit the identity of Rolls for the sake of the BMW brand so it can build cars that might compete in a higher price segment with Bentley 99.

It was no coincidence that Pischetrieder referred to the iconographic status of Rolls. For him Rolls was the final piece in the upmarket portfolio that represented his vision of BMW. In this respect, he and Reitzle were at one: their goals were always compatible; only their strategies conflicted.

Hurricane Sterling

But even as BMW celebrated one of its most conspicuous triumphs – with its Rolls-Royce coup being hailed on both sides of the Atlantic – the seeds of disaster which had been sown at Rover were about to sprout. BMW was about to reap the whirlwind. It was a financial whirlwind, and if whirlwinds were named like hurricanes, this one would have been called Sterling.

Early in 1995, the pound had bottomed out after its long decline following Britain's withdrawal from the European Union's Exchange Rate Mechanism (ERM). Against the Deutschmark, it edged up during 1995 and then took off. Sterling, which had averaged DM2.35 during 1996, climbed by the end of 1997 to DM2.90, having exceeded DM3 in July and August. For Pischetsrieder, Luderitz and Hasselkus, whose long-term planning for Rover **BMW was about to reap the whirlwind** was on the basis of a worst-case scenario of DM2.62–DM2.68, sterling's rise spelled trouble with a capital T. Temporarily, Rover was insulated against the currency's appreciation, because until June 1998 its sales to mainland Europe were hedged at about DM2.40.

But once the hedge ran out, unless the pound dropped significantly in the meantime, Rover would be terribly exposed to a double whammy: the already slim margins on its exports to Europe – which accounted for almost the entire overseas sales of Rover cars – would be wiped out, while at home it would be spreadeagled in the face of continental rivals who were already using the headroom provided by the relative decline of their currencies to cut their British prices. This scenario immediately jeopardized BMW's stated timetable for returning Rover to profit in 2000. That, in turn, would hit the share price – and a rocky share price would turn up the heat on Pischetsrieder's strategy. The BMW chairman was aware of the problem. As early as 1996, he forecast on BBC Radio that: 'Britain will have to join the euro in order to reduce the value of the pound.'

Like the captain in *The Poseidon Adventure*, who could only watch helplessly from the bridge as the giant tidal wave rolled towards him, Hasselkus too could see what was coming. He said in September 1997: 'It's sometimes difficult to separate your long-term direction from the short-term problems – the investment costs, the impact of the strong pound. You lose money and then people ask, "Are you going to make it? Will you break even in 2000 (BMW's original plan)?" The answer to that,' he continued, 'is yes, but only if the pound doesn't stay strong for the next couple of years. None of this should take away from the clear vision and strategy we are following. We are determined to start a new era for Rover.'

Pischetrieder's and Hasselkus's hopes for Rover were firmly pinned on the 600/800 replacement, codenamed RD1. As the codename implied, RD1 was the first model to be developed entirely since the takeover. Later recoded R40, it was due to be launched at the October 1998 Birmingham international motor show. According to Hasselkus, 'All new Rover products are equally important.' However, R40 was more important than others. Until 1999, when R40 hit the market, all the moves by Hasselkus and Purves to revitalize Rover would be inevitably limited by the lack of new, BMW-inspired products.

R40 was to be the cornerstone of BMW's attempt to revive the brand values once associated with Rover. Hasselkus said: 'Rover was an upmarket car for doctors, lawyers and other professionals. The centre of gravity of the brand is now lower than it used to be because of the type of models we have. For general and strategic reasons, we believe we should position the centre of gravity of the brand higher upmarket.' Hasselkus believed the world was waiting for a truly British car, despite the irony that it would be a German company that financed it. John Towers once described the essence of Britishness as 'performance without stress'. That is probably the most accurate description of the legacy left by the upper echelons of the British class system, and is almost a definition of amateurism. But that was what Rover had come to epitomize.

Hasselkus's view, after first seeing what became the Rover 75, was that: 'The proof of the pudding is in the eating. Will we be able to launch something where the public at large says: "That is a beautiful British car"?

That is a challenge I am absolutely convinced we are able to meet. I'm not nervous at all. The car is fantastic. I would lay an awful lot of my private money on its success and that is saying something, because I am not a gambler.'

Hasselkus had confused three separate issues. First, would they produce a beautiful car? Answer: certainly. Second, would the public love it? Answer: probably. Third, would it be a success of the size that Rover needed? Answer: probably not. Luckily for Hasselkus, nobody took his bet.

BMW reckoned the car, codenamed R40, would compete at the upper end of its price range with Jaguar's S-type, and lower down the range with Volvo and Audi – although both Jaguar and Audi were starting to attack the sporty, dynamic segment dominated by BMW. A later version of R40 was also to be the spearhead of Rover's planned return to the American car market. Already some analysts were calling R40 Rover's 'last chance saloon'. Stephen Reitman, European motors analyst at Merrill Lynch, was just one of many analysts who saw R40 as make or break. He said: 'R40's significance cannot be overestimated as BMW's whole strategy of where it wants to take Rover cars as a counterpoint to the BMW brand will be put under the microscope.'

Moment of Truth

The final countdown to Rover's moment of truth began on Wednesday 20 May 1998. The company announced it would create 1000 direct jobs at Cowley, now renamed Rover Oxford, as it geared up for the launch, with another 5000 being created among suppliers. That would increase the Oxford workforce by almost 50 per cent, from 2500 to 3500. BMW had invested £250m to equip Oxford to build the car Pischetsrieder and his allies wanted. A new paint plant, with capacity to produce 250,000 cars a year, was the fulcrum of the revamped factory and an indicator of Rover's long-term ambitions to make Oxford a multi-model plant.

The R40 assembly line itself – which Rover called 'a factory within a factory' – had been meticulously planned to ensure that the car set new standards for Rover in terms of build quality, reliability and durability; in other words, to BMW standards. Quite reasonably Hasselkus commented, 'We have put our money where our mouth is. We have invested where it really counts.' Perhaps it would have been more accurate to say that BMW had invested where it should have counted. Doug Dickson, managing director of the Oxford plant, was equally buoyant. He said that Rover would maximize the return on BMW's substantial investment in R40. 'Capital productivity is vital. We are making the assets sweat through introducing flexible shifts – we have agreements that could enable us to run the plant throughout the year – and through establishing close relationships between engineering and the shopfloor.' A BMW-devised system called QZ would enable shopfloor managers to obtain instant feedback from dealers about customer reaction, enabling rapid removal of any faults that escaped the rigorous Q quality system which Rover had adopted from BMW.

Quality was no longer a sufficient differentiator in a world where brand is king

Rover used to quality check cars in 75 minutes; under QZ it takes a day. In body assembly, 85 per cent of the work would be done by robots, against 70 per cent on the 600 and 800. Apart from working closely with BMW engineers, Rover also scoured the UK for production experts, bringing in people from Nissan in Sunderland, Toyota in Derby and Motorola in Scotland – and sent staff to Kawasaki in Japan to view the latest techniques.

The aim was to breed a true culture of continuous improvement, something the group lacked despite years of co-operation with Honda. 'We are not trying to change the world overnight,' said Dickson. 'We are aiming to do it step by step.' However, the significance of the car went much further than job numbers. It was, as Rover pointed out, the 'first all-new Rover executive car designed and engineered in Britain for more than 25 years'. Every executive model since the ill-fated SD1 had been developed with or derived from Honda. R40 was clearly going to be a good-looking, well-furnished car. However, as Reitzle knew, quality was no longer a sufficient differentiator in a world where brand is king. Nor was value the only concern; volume was an issue as well.

The expectations set for what the company accurately described as 'the first all-new Rover executive car designed and engineered in Britain for more than 25 years' were forbidding. First, it needed to reach high sales targets. In its first year, 1999, Rover aimed to sell 90,000 cars – almost double Oxford's 1998 output as the 600 and 800 ran out. In 2000, its first full year, BMW had now reduced its original aim of selling 140,000 R40s to 120,000 – still very high for a model in this segment of the market, where sales of 70,000–80,000 a year were usual. But if the targets could be hit, the efficiency benefits would be enormous: output per head at Oxford would be doubled over the 1998 level.

The geographical balance of those sales was also planned to be very different from that of the 75's predecessors, about 85 per cent of which had been sold in Britain. About 70 per cent of the 75s were to go overseas, mainly to continental Europe, with only 30 per cent sold in Britain. Within five years, BMW planned to launch the 75 in America, alongside other Rover group models such as the new Mini. Germany was the largest single target market. 'Rover was almost forgotten in Germany,' said Hasselkus. There, Rover had increased sales from a tiny 8000 in 1993 to 32,000 in 1997 – still only 1 per cent of Europe's biggest car market.

Under the halo created by R40, Hasselkus believed the marque could raise annual sales there to 120,000 vehicles. There was some evidence that Hasselkus's claim was more than hype when one hard-bitten City dealer, in the wake of Daimler-Benz's £55 billion merger with America's Chrysler, said 'They are talking about how Chrysler could benefit in Europe from the Rover–BMW effect.' The argument was that 'since the BMW takeover, Rover's attraction for continental buyers ha[d] been hugely enhanced'. Pischetsrieder and Hasselkus may have taken that as a backhanded compliment, because the effective takeover of Chrysler by Jurgen Schrempp's Daimler in May 1998 left BMW isolated as a European maker of premium cars.

Through the rose-coloured glasses the duo seemed to be wearing, they saw the isolation as splendid. 'We are now the only exclusive car manufacturing group in the world,' said Hasselkus. The deal had the curious side effect of creating the first ever formal joint venture between BMW and its arch-rival Mercedes, because DaimlerChrysler now inherited the Brazil engine factory which was to supply Mini. That, however, was incidental. For BMW, the nub of the deal, which sparked huge and widespread consolidation in the world car industry, was to remove the possibility of a

Chrysler–Rover alliance. BMW's turnaround effort at Rover had just become a high-wire act without a safety net. 'Failure with Rover was never an option,' said the laconic Hasselkus. 'But the Daimler-Chrysler merger makes success even more important, if that's possible.'

Would the public buy the image of Rover that the designers and marketeers wanted to sell? Geoff Upex, Rover's design director, said that the most important thing they had done with the 75 was to 'design the Britishness back into our cars', after the long association with Honda had eroded it. With the 75, he argued, the challenge was to find the balance between 'heritage and modernity. We want the car to refer back to an era of more crafted products'. Widespread use of chrome and retro interior styling helped to evoke the premium brand values the Rover marque represented in the 1950s and 1960s, while abundant use of twenty-first century technology updated the image. The car was positioned squarely in the 'comfort and refinement' segment of the premium market.

Hopes were high. 'R40 can take us a long way,' said Purves, the man responsible for masterminding the rebranding programme. 'We can reasonably expect a cascade of positive effect from the big car to the smaller cars, just as the introduction of the new BMW 5 series helped sell the 3 series.' Hasselkus was confident that the 75 would deliver. 'It will start a new era for Rover cars,' he said. 'For me, it is the contemporary interpretation of what Rover once stood for. The car has heritage, but it is also modern. It is also different, in a very elegant and classy way, from everything else in this segment.' Rarely in the modern motor industry had so much been riding on a single product. For Rover, its Munich parent, and to a certain extent the British economy, the months leading to its launch were going to be a truly defining period.

Nobody believed that the model, invested with much of BMW's technical and marketing know-how, as well as £400m of its cash plus the £250m on Oxford, would flop. More accurately, nobody dared to believe it. However, even partial success was not going to be enough to revitalize the flagging Rover marque. There had to be complete success. The car had to be an outright hit. 'The R40 is vital for the Rover car business,' said Hasselkus with acquired British understatement.

To attain premium status, however, Rover needed more models. One of them was to be the new Mini, due to be launched as a separate brand in

2001. But BMW was already revising down price and volume expectations for the car, which in any case was to be sold through Rover dealers only in Britain. BMW dealers were to handle it everywhere else. For Rover, the most crucial project was the medium-sized car, codenamed R30, which would slot in below the 75, replacing the Rover 200 and Rover 400. Rover thought it could sell 350,000 of these cars a year. Both R30 and Mini were to be produced at Longbridge, where BMW planned to invest £1bn over the next four years, plus £400m on the R30 and £400m on Mini – around £1.8bn in total.

10

Did the Earth Move For You?

VEN AS HASSELKUS AND HIS TEAM geared up for the 75 launch at Birmingham and looked ahead to the Longbridge redevelopment, the ground beneath them was moving. In March 1998 the pound had hit DM3.10. Although it subsequently declined slightly, it was still standing at more than DM2.70 as the key registration month of August approached in Britain. Rover's currency hedge fell away in June. The company was now fully and painfully exposed to the pound's appreciation. The impact on sales exceeded by far even the worst fears of Rover insiders. 'From the start of July, sales simply went off a cliff,' said one executive.

Another former executive said the sales planning process went wrong. 'They believed they were going to sell more than 500,000 vehicles – about the same as last year – but the exchange rate changed all that. Peugeot, Renault, Fiat and Volkswagen have had a bonanza in Britain,' he said. On 23 July, with the motor show less than three months away, Hasselkus was driven to announce bad news. Rover was cutting at least 1500 jobs and putting workers on some of its product lines on a four-day week. The statement was headed: 'Rover Group moves to counter overvalued pound'. In it Hasselkus revealed the level of underlying concern:

    ❝❝ We have been protected from the effects of the strong pound by forward buying of currency, but this protection cannot last forever. The time has come when we must take action. Although our productivity has improved significantly in the last few years, it cannot compensate for the distortion in trading conditions caused by the 30 per cent decrease in sterling competitiveness since

1996. At a time when Rover Group's exports are increasing, the negative effect of currency on our business is considerable. The service and financial sectors of the UK economy give a false impression of what is happening in the real world of manufacturing and international competitiveness. The current value of the pound means our revenue from vehicles sold abroad is reduced, while cheap imports are sucked into our home market ❞❞.

Such statements did not endear Hasselkus to the Labour government. Even those political arch-enemies Gordon Brown, the chancellor, and Peter Mandelson, trade and industry secretary, were united in rejecting Rover's currency complaints. They both blamed the company for not doing enough to raise productivity. They were both wrong. While Rover had scope to increase efficiency, productivity was not its main problem. As the largest British exporter to continental Europe by a mile (or a kilometre) – Rover's sales to the mainland were three times the size of the next largest exporter – the company was uniquely exposed to sterling's surge.

The company was uniquely exposed to sterling's surge

One obvious route to mitigate the impact of the high pound was to buy more overseas components. BMW had started this process with the 75, which had a 70–75 per cent UK content rather than Rover's habitual 85 per cent. But here, as in other respects, the pound's rise cruelly penalized BMW both for the time it had taken to bring through new Rover models and the choices it had made for that model programme.

BMW had run a calculated risk in deferring replacement of the 200 and 400, which accounted for more than three-quarters of its cars output, until 2002. It reckoned that with facelifts of the two models in 1999 it could keep their sales rolling long enough to tide the company over until a new model, code named R30, was ready to carry Rover into the premium segment in the middle market, just as the 75 was doing in the executive sector. The 200 and 400 prices would have to be cut, but BMW reckoned volume could be maintained in Britain and grown in mainland Europe to compensate for the decline in revenue per vehicle.

The pound's rise blew that fragile strategy apart. In Germany, where BMW hoped sales of the 200 and 400 could be grown, the 400 base model sold for DM29,000 before the upsurge in sterling. The pound's rise drove the cost up to DM39,000 – far out of line with the competition. Rover had no choice but to start loading up the cars with specification and cutting prices, but on top of that it had to support sales both at home and overseas with heavy spending on marketing. Sterling also delivered a third blow: its rise inflated Rover's losses in Deutschmark terms. Of course, what was bad news for Rover was excellent news for BMW. It was about to break the 60,000 sales barrier in Britain, and the profitability of those sales was enormously enhanced by the Deutschmark's fall. That fact was frequently ignored in the months to come, as Rover's losses exploded. In a perverse way, the effect in Germany was the reverse: in the minds of many, the currency changes pushed BMW and Rover further apart, strengthening the case for dumping 'the English Patient', as Rover now became nicknamed after the film of that title. That psychology also began to penetrate the BMW supervisory board.

Rover had cut its losses to £91m in 1997. Now, those losses were ballooning. It looked as if they might exceed £500m for the full year. For Pischetsrieder, that was intolerable and unsustainable. Four weeks before the motor show, Pischetsrieder slammed on the brakes. All investment at Longbridge, on Mini and on R30 was frozen. 'The shareholders of BMW can't be prepared to spend money on a business which has no positive outlook,' he said later. Behind the scenes, the government and union leaders were quietly told about the crisis. But publicly, BMW wanted to do nothing that would cloud the 75's motor show launch. First thing on Tuesday, 20 October, to the accompaniment of a specially composed fanfare played by the London Symphony Orchestra, Hasselkus unveiled the Rover 75.

A powder blue car, its lines of chrome gleaming in the arena arc lights, descended on a mechanized gantry in front of a horde of media watchers, Rover personnel and union leaders. It was an impressive debut. Privately, however, BMW executives had other matters on their mind. That lunchtime, one confided to an associate that the strength of the pound was causing havoc at Rover. He laid the blame squarely on the government: 'The level of the pound is ridiculous,' he said. 'It should be at DM2.50. They are killing manufacturing industry.'

Balloon Goes Up

The balloon finally went up just before 4.30 that afternoon, in the cavernous Hall 17 on the outer reaches of the National Exhibition Centre where the biennial show is held. BMW had scheduled its group press conference there, but the event was expected to be routine and so late in the day was the meeting that some journalists had already left the show. They missed one hell of a story. The conference was due to start at 4 pm, but the minutes ticked by as Pischetsrieder, Hasselkus and Richard Gaul, BMW's corporate affairs chief, huddled round a small table, discussing the final shape of Pischetsrieder's address. Across the room, Ludcritz and Runnacles watched and waited.

Eventually Pischetsrieder took the stage. What he said shook Britain's car industry to its roots, along with swathes of Whitehall, Westminster and the West Midlands. His message was that Rover was in crisis. 'Short-term actions are required for the long-term future of the Rover group,' said Pischetsrieder. 'Talks are taking place with the British government about the whole problem.' The message BMW had quietly delivered to both the government and the unions was stark: Longbridge was economically unviable. Unless costs were cut by hundreds of millions of pounds, several thousand jobs shed and sweeping improvements to job flexibility achieved, BMW would have to close it. 'Only if those three elements – cost cuts, productivity improvements and government aid – were in place,' said Pischetsrieder, would the Mini and R30 proceed.

Some time later, after he had left BMW, Pischetsrieder described his reasoning behind the shock announcement:

> ❝ BMW culture is that you try to solve your problems inside the company and not to talk about it in public. This has always been the BMW way at least until the very last months. It was always very successful but it was not, to the same extent, successful within Rover. So I decided that I needed to give this problem a sort of public background. It had to be *on* stage and not just *behind* stage in order to get things moving ❞.

Well, the announcement certainly did that. Pischetsrieder pulled no punches. He said, bluntly: 'With these products, the future of Longbridge will be secure. Without them, there will be no plant. We have made good progress with Rover, but it is not enough,' he continued. 'The parameters under which we planned the next couple of years for Rover have changed.'

Among those shifting parameters, one stood above all others in Pischetsrieder's view. The pound's surge had sent Rover hurtling towards bottom-line losses that were now projected to be £600m for the year. In its Herculean effort to remake Rover, BMW had left its toughest and costliest tasks, both in plant and product, until last: the attempt to create a premium-priced, middle-market car that could compete with VW's Golf, and the complete overhaul of the sprawling hulk that was Longbridge.

> **'The reason Longbridge has never made any money is nothing to do with unit productivity,' said Bhatta charyya. 'The plant is simply too big'**

For decades, the factory that Herbert Austin bought for £7750 in 1905 had cast a giant shadow over Rover. In recent years, that had not been because Longbridge's 14,000 workers – 8500 on car assembly, 5500 making engines – had fallen down on the job. In fact, as Warwick University's Bhattacharyya said: 'Rover as a whole, including Longbridge, has made a remarkable recovery in manufacturing terms. Productivity has increased year by year.' Comparisons with factories such as Nissan in Sunderland were erroneous according to Bhattacharyya: 'They are green-field sites, purpose-designed for late 20th-century car-making and built on a modular basis so their capacity can be aligned to demand.' Longbridge, by contrast, was the brownest of brown-field plants, a site that had been starved of the investment which would allow it to be modernized and streamlined. 'The reason Longbridge has never made any money is nothing to do with unit productivity,' said Bhattacharyya. 'The plant is simply too big.'

Bhattacharyya said: 'Longbridge has been starved of investment since the Metro was launched in 1980. Nothing has been done there since, except on an ad hoc basis. One reason Rover Cars has never made money is because it has never achieved the volumes intended. Even the Metro fell short of planned sales.' Such statements reinforced the view of many experts that BMW had been reckless in its decision to buy Rover and try to run with all of the sites. To make a return, Longbridge needed to produce 450,000 cars a year; the previous year it made fewer than 340,000. But together, the Mini and R30 would deliver the volume. The question now was: could BMW afford to build R30 and renovate Longbridge.

In a nod to the government's argument that Rover was inefficient, Pischetsrieder emphasized the need to close what he said was a 30 per cent gap in value added per worker between Rover and BMW. 'We have progressively cut the gap from 50 per cent when we took over, but given the pressure from the market and the exchange rate, we have to cut deeper and faster,' he said.

Much of the gap was due to the difference in working practices between German and British factories. BMW's more flexible working arrangements allowed greater capital productivity in BMW's home plants. However, such agreements had already been rejected by Rover unions when first proposed in the summer. It was clear that BMW had made great progress in getting flexible working in Germany and was extremely annoyed when the British would not go along. But another reason for the value added disparity was the simple fact that BMW cars' premium prices meant unit margins were higher than at Longbridge in particular.

Until the new cars came in, Longbridge was in a vicious circle. To close the value added gap, it needed the new models that were to establish Rover as a premium brand and increase the unit value of each car. Unless and until BMW took its foot off the investment brake, Longbridge could not fulfil BMW's strategic vision for Rover. Whether Longbridge lived or died, therefore, depended on three interlinked entities: the BMW board, Rover's unions and 39,000-strong workforce, and the British government.

Unions and workforce had responded positively to BMW's push for 'burden-sharing' cost savings, including up to 3000 job cuts and more flexible manning arrangements. The company wanted to save £450m over three years – almost half the cost of its Longbridge investment programme; £150m of that was to be pay related savings.

To make the sums add up to the satisfaction of the supervisory board, Pischetsrieder also needed government aid for the new models, particularly the R30. Ministers, some of whom had initially dismissed Rover's complaints about the impact of sterling, belatedly came to appreciate that

BMW was in earnest. Mandelson, for example, realized that there was a faction at BMW which wanted to close Longbridge and walk away from Rover. BMW wanted about £200m from the government, which was reckoned to be ready to provide about half that sum. In the fraught negotiating climate which existed at the time there was little room for error. Pischetsrieder told Mandelson that a decision on Longbridge had to be made by the end of November.

Failing a satisfactory outcome, BMW would move the Mini to Oxford and start Longbridge's rundown. The BMW chief knew what was at stake. 'It will be extremely painful to eliminate the value-added gap, but it has to be achieved for the sake of the future of the entire business, not just for Rover but for the supplier industry in Britain,' he said. One Longbridge worker was more succinct: 'We've got to change or Longbridge goes bust. And if that happens, the Midlands goes bust.'

There was one immediate casualty of Pischetsrieder's doomsday announcement. The news completely scuttled the 75 launch. As a result, BMW's revelation of the threat to Longbridge – and therefore to Rover – blighted the very model designed to spark Rover's recovery from that crisis. The normally sure-footed BMW's decision to go public about Longbridge mystified its rivals: 'They have shot themselves in both feet,' said the chairman of one big car company. 'I can't understand it.'

What was not mystifying was Rover's insistence that the workforce must accept new flexible working patterns similar to those operating at BMW. These required staff to work longer or shorter hours depending on demand, and fewer but longer shifts to maximize the use of plant and return on investment. The BMW board also demanded an acceleration of the integration of BMW and Rover operations, particularly on joint procurement of components. The decision to admit problems publicly was seen as a tacit admission that the German company should have moved further and faster in integrating the operations. It also emerged that BMW had considered a deal with its rival Volkswagen, which would have involved adapting the Golf platform to develop the medium-sized Rover model. But a satisfactory government aid package would make such a deal unnecessary.

It was anticipated that state aid for Longbridge, which was eligible for regional selective assistance, would almost certainly be approved by the

European Commission since it had previously cleared hefty packages for Jaguar and General Motors' Vauxhall subsidiary, as well as about £40m in aid for BMW's Hams Hall engine plant. None of those projects, however, approached the economic, employment or, especially, political significance of Longbridge to the West Midlands. The region's enterprise board estimated that almost 60,000 jobs were dependent on the plant, including the 14,000 people directly employed and more than 45,000 among component and services suppliers.

11 The Holy Grail

NDER PISCHETSRIEDER'S PLAN, suppliers would be asked to reduce prices by at least 10 per cent during the course of 1999, while the 39,000 Rover workers were expected to be cut by 3000, mostly at Longbridge. The Transport & General Workers Union immediately brought in Peter Regnier, a former Rover finance director, to carry out its own audit of BMW's complex cost-reduction proposals. Rover's most pressing need, both to impress its German owners and to win over the government, was to gain union agreement to the radical improvements in flexible working. No one underestimated the extent of the changes the Rover workforce was being asked to accept. One BMW executive said: 'Because of the sterling situation, we have to ask our Rover colleagues to do in one year what it took our German workers 12 years to accept.'

Fortunately, a strong bond existed between the British unions and the BMW supervisory board: Tony Woodley and Manfred Schoch were close friends. Woodley was TGWU motor industry national negotiator and chairman of the union side of the car industry joint negotiating committee and Schoch was chairman of the BMW works council and deputy chairman of the supervisory board. Woodley was a long serving union man who had reinvented himself as a 'new Labour' unionist and Schoch was unusually highly placed on the supervisory board as well as being a 'union' representative.

Hasselkus's initial inclination was to terminate all existing Rover contracts and then to re-employ less staff on flexible shift patterns. The unions, particularly Woodley, resisted from the outset. He convinced Hasselkus and even some of his own wavering union colleagues that, given the enormity of the changes BMW wanted, it was essential to gain the support of the bulk of the workforce. The story of the union–management negotiations, as told by Woodley, reveals the complex matrix of personal and organizational relationships that ran through the BMW–Rover marriage.

There were not, for example, simply two players – unions and management – there were divisions within the unions and divisions within in the management. In the unions there were those who kept urging Woodley to 'take 'em on'. But Woodley knew that merely taking them on was not a viable option. As he said, 'The game had changed from the 1970s, and this was a unique, massive problem. Confrontation wasn't appropriate because BMW wasn't bluffing' However, he also believed that rolling over was not an option either. What was needed was finesse.

On the management side there was also division. The Rover management were in desperate straits and opted for a sledge-hammer approach, whereas their BMW counterparts were less **What was needed was finesse** sure and willing to be more accommodating. Rover directors, therefore, came to the unions and said that there needed to be huge wage-related cuts and the unions would have to forego their upcoming wage rises. At the time the parties were only one year into a three-year deal which had been painstakingly negotiated precisely to stabilize wage costs for planning purposes. It was also only four months after about 1200 forced redundancies of temporary workers. Woodley, against the general union feeling, which was becoming fatalistic in the face of the setbacks, rejected the wage cut demands, arguing that an acceptance would send the wrong signals to an already demoralized workforce as well as to a belligerent management.

The rejection had two immediate consequences. First, 'it seriously pissed off the Rover directors' and second, 'it strengthened the workforce'. Now Woodley takes up the story himself:

> ❝ At the end of the day I still had the problem, how do we get from A to B with £150m worth of wage-related savings which we'd promised Pischetsrieder a week earlier. We'd met him privately, said to him, 'We're prepared to help because there's only one game in town for Rover and that's called the Pischetsrieder plan ❞.

> ❝ He had bought Rover, he had a plan for Rover, he was prepared to fulfil his obligations to Rover and, unlike many companies beforehand, BMW had put its money where its mouth was. They had invested £2.5bn, they wanted to invest more. But if Pischetsrieder fell, as indeed was the plot by Reitzle behind the scenes, then the game was up for Rover, it was certainly up for Longbridge that's for sure ❞.

> ❝ If Reitzle had won, Longbridge was gone – there was no middle ground. The Reitzle plan was to close Rover cars ❞.

To save Rover meant delivering the £150m wage-related savings the unions had promised Pischetsrieder, but they had to do it while retaining the wage deal as it stood. Then, as Woodley put it:

> ❝ We had some luck. It was a Saturday night, it had been a long, knackering week with Rover and we'd rejected their pay freeze demands. Saturday is my football day and I was on my way back from football and I thought, 'I'll give Manfred [Schoch] a ring.' 'Manfred, just to bring you up to speed me old mate, took a gamble today. I've told 'em, no. The wage rise is going ahead, its going to be announced Monday ❞.

This was an extraordinary conversation to have occurred between the union negotiator for Rover workers and the deputy chairman of the supervisory board of Rover's parent company. The fact that Schoch was also the works council representative only added to the unique mixture. Having told Schoch he had decided to continue with the wage increase demand, Woodley said:

> ❝ I believe rejection is the right move but I'm in trouble now, because I've got to find that £150m from somewhere else and there's not many big opportunities for that sort of money ❞.

Then the breakthrough happened. Schoch asked Woodley whether he had thought about 'hours' as the answer. Woodley assumed that he meant the sort of reduction in hours and wages that VW had agreed at Wolfsburg a couple of years earlier. Woodley responded that he had actually tried that before (in July) when the redundancies of temp workers were imminent and it had not been well received by the unions then, let alone the management. Schoch explained that what he meant was actually reducing the working week. By introducing a more flexible working arrangement in which hours would be banked and used by both sides as appropriate to demand, it might be possible to deliver up the holy grail of British industrial relations – a 35-hour week.

Despite Schoch's enthusiasm, Woodley said, 'There's one thing for sure, these Rover directors won't have that.' Schoch listened to Woodley's concerns and asked whether he had any objections if Schoch floated the idea with BMW. Schoch believed it was a runner because if the unions agreed to delay, by a year, taking the shorter working week, there would be a straight gain on capital and the one thing BMW needed was money.

Schoch returned from his consultations and said that BMW was willing to try to get an agreement along the lines proposed. For Woodley that was when things got 'incredibly hairy'. The reason was that only Woodley knew that the negotiation machinery was on the move. All sides had agreed to reconvene the following week and yet behind the scene things were happening. At this point the still uninformed David Bower, personnel director of Rover, came to Woodley with what amounted to an ultimatum. As reported by Woodley, Bower said:

> 66 Look, Mr Woodley, you say you're prepared to be helpful but we've had more than 20 meetings with you and still no agreement. If by 23 November there is still no agreement, then it will be our intention to give notice to the total workforce, to sack the workforce, to reduce their wages and terms and conditions 99.

Woodley said that Bower's list was a litany of costs and reductions. 'Reduce premiums, the removal of sick pay schemes, the sacking of people. You name it they attacked it. To get the value.' Woodley continued:

> 66 As I reported back to the members, the question was – is this someone trying it on, or are these people serious with the hope that you'll keel over

and give them part of that? And the reality of it was, they wanted all of that. And that was real, real pressure. Even the strongest characters on our side [union], you could hear the intake of breath, the shock when it hit them. I always knew they weren't joking but the others didn't. They thought they were trying it on. Now they knew. Four days later I went to the office again and said to the union officers, 'Sit down, I have a cunning plan. I believe there's a way in which we can help the company and at the same time get something out of this for our members as opposed to just conceding wage-related cost cuts. I think we can get a 35-hour week out of this.' Well, if they'd been shocked by the company's attitude they were doubly shocked with this lunatic – I can remember one person who said 'Tony this is getting f*****g ridiculous, you're going to take our people up a hill here and never bring them down again.' I then said to them, 'Excuse me gents you're missing the point. I'm not saying I think, I'm saying, we've got a deal.' Because the deal had been struck with BMW directors behind the backs of Rover 🙿🙿.

The officers were just not sure and finally Woodley asked them to simply trust him. With their grudging acceptance, Woodley and the other officers travelled to meet with the management negotiators. Under the German system, Hasselkus was nominally only the chairman and the company had others to do the negotiating – including David Bower as the chief negotiator for Rover. By sheer good fortune, Hasselkus came into the room to talk about something else entirely. He certainly was not there to negotiate. However, while he was there Woodley took the opportunity to put his plan to the chairman.

Woodley reports that he then said, 'Walter, a few days ago we were accused of not being specific with our proposals, I now have a firm proposal to put to you.' As Woodley said, 'I then ran through the plan – £1.5bn of investment, model confirmation, no enforced redundancies, we would do this, this, this, this and this.' Hasselkus, surrounded by his dumbstruck negotiators, could only say, 'Well all we can do, Tony, is take your proposals away and look at them.' They were away six hours. They returned without Hasselkus. Bower said, 'It's quite obvious Mr Woodley you've been incredibly busy behind the scenes.'

'Quite simply,' said Woodley, 'they'd been kebabed, they'd been outma-noeuvred.' They were, to coin Woodley's phrase, 'totally Schoch-ed'. The cunning plan had unforeseen consequences. The Rover team was affronted by what appeared to them as an ignominious defeat. They did everything within their power to convince the German management that the plan should not, could not, be allowed to happen. Simultaneously, the unions were saying to the Germans that 'if this deal is unacceptable then you will get nothing more from us'.

Over the next eight or nine days the unions were working feverishly to flesh out the details of the deal. By contrast, the Rover management was doing nothing because its only plan had been to cut the wages or sack the workers – they had no alternative strategies on which to work. The evening after the meeting, Woodley was in the bar of the conference centre when he saw, on the Nine O' Clock News, an announcement that Rover and the unions had reached an agreement to 'work Saturdays'. MSF, one of the minor union players, had let slip what it thought were the details of a done deal. Rather than having a 'done' deal, the unions were still in deep trouble. Woodley arranged a meeting with three main Rover directors, the manufacturing director, the personnel director (David Bower) and one other.

The manufacturing director said that they were not against the union's proposals, they simply 'couldn't manage it'. Woodley said:

> ❝ I leaned forward and said, 'Gentlemen, there's a time in life when people should listen, and I'm telling you, the three of you, you listen to what I'm telling you now. If you don't listen to me you're going to get the sack. And I'll tell you why. You're telling me you can't manage change. If you can't manage change, which is two hours a week, in Germany the owners of this company manage five hours a week flexibility. If you tell them, what you're telling me – that you can't manage it – then they will assume they've got the wrong men for the job. Because we've reached a deal using the deputy chairman of the supervisory board whose value to BMW is ten times the value of you. Do you think they're going to scupper him to save you? You're gambling with your jobs. You're gonna lose. Listen to me, get the deal done and dusted and signed ❞.

They didn't listen and they lost their jobs. There was still some hard bargaining to be done which is where the Saturday working leak came from. The unions had a prize (the 35-hour week) and the Rover management wanted its prize, which turned out to be compulsory Saturday working. Woodley recalled how they made their offer:

> 66 They came to me on the last minute of the last day and said, 'Mr Woodley, I'm instructed to inform you, from the BMW directors, that there will be no agreement reached, unless you agree to compulsory Saturday working.' My answer was quite simple, 'Bollocks! That's one step too far 99.

He said he had taken the stand not to be awkward but because he judged that his members simply would not have stood for such an agreement. Woodley refused to move on that point and faxed Schoch with the unions' final position, which did not include compulsory Saturday workings. Schoch did some more work and the next day all parties met. The BMW directors and union officials agreed on a few final points of dispute and then, along with the Rover directors, thus presented the proposed agreement to Pischetsrieder. The deal was done.

'If I hadn't seen what I've just seen, I would never have believed it.'

Woodley recalled that Bower emerged from the meeting and said: 'If I hadn't seen what I've just seen, I would never have believed it.' What he'd seen was the unions, both German and British, in complete unity and working with the BMW chairman to find a solution which would save the company, even if the pride of the Rover directors had to suffer.

Under the ground-breaking framework agreed by BMW and the unions, over two years a Rover employee's working week would fall from five shifts totalling 37 hours to one of four shifts totalling 35 hours. Simultaneously the 1999 and 2000 pay rises would be reduced, at a stroke also reducing capital costs. Costs would be cut without any compulsory redundancies.

CHAPTER **12** **The Evaluation**

THE DEAL STRUCK BETWEEN BMW AND THE UNIONS was so unique that, as soon as it was announced, Pischetsrieder had a call from Ford's Jac Nasser, asking him, 'How the hell did you manage it?' Despite its uniqueness, however, and the lack of 'compulsory' redundancies, there was nonetheless one extremely significant 'voluntary' redundancy. On 2 December 1998, Walter Hasselkus announced his resignation as chairman and chief executive of Rover. Ironically, the announcement of the agreement with the unions came on that same December day.

Hasselkus's achievement with the unions had, in fact, been little short of miraculous. Inside two months he had managed to agree terms which had taken more than a decade and a bitter six-week strike to achieve in Germany. As one senior manager said, 'We didn't want to have to teach our colleagues at Rover in one week what we have taught our colleagues in Germany over 12 years, but we had to.'

Hasselkus said he was resigning because of Rover's spiralling losses. Flanked by Pischetsrieder and Woodley, Hasselkus signed off with regret – and a typical aside: 'This is a very difficult and painful process for me, not least because I'm emotionally very much attached to Rover Group and to the Rover associates.' Then he joked: 'I even learnt to like Tony Woodley.' But as he fell on his sword, Sir Walter made one final piercing thrust:

> ❝❝ BMW has a very strong corporate culture and believes in individual and entrepreneurial responsibility. Rover Group's performance has been influenced by quite a number of factors completely beyond our control. But

we simply got it wrong in not anticipating the fierceness of the competition in the British market. So when I came around 360 degrees and looked at myself, I felt quite strongly that somebody had to stand up and be counted 🙶🙶.

Hasselkus did not leave a bare cupboard. For one thing, there was the ground-breaking union deal that could underpin BMW's commitment to

Hasselkus did not leave a bare cupboard

future model development. With the new working system and new models, BMW would have strengthened the foundations for its plan to turn Rover into a premium brand. Hasselkus's resignation and his replacement by Werner Samann, 56, a BMW veteran who headed the engines and suspension division, signified an equally fundamental shift to a more hands-on approach by BMW.

With Rover's losses soaring as the world car market slowed, the question was whether BMW had moved too late to prevent the Viking longship from sinking. Samann, a technologist, was the embodiment of the tightening operational links between Munich and Rover after the appointment of Christian John von Freyend, BMW's former financial controller, as Rover's finance director.

Up to 100 BMW engineers were, by that stage, playing key roles inside Rover. Many were working at Oxford to repair the quality problems that had already put the new Rover 75 executive model eight weeks behind schedule for its planned March launch. Many believed that greater Munich involvement was long overdue. Bhattacharyya said: 'If they had taken charge at an earlier stage, these things might not have gone wrong or at least BMW would have reacted faster. Instead, the situation got out of control this year.'

The flexible working practice changes still had to be accepted by the Rover workers, 27,000 of whom were bussed to Birmingham's National Exhibition Centre to learn about the survival plan. They were being asked for a change of mindset, abandoning working patterns established for decades. The changes were designed to enable BMW to run plants for 102 hours a week, instead of 74. Acceptance of the package was by no means guaranteed. There was, for example, considerable rivalry between Rover factories and opposition to the new deal was evident at Cowley and

Solihull. The Swindon body plant was less of an issue, since its fate was clearly tied to that of Longbridge.

Cowley, in particular, saw Longbridge's crisis as a case of the biter bit. The antique divide between Morris and Austin died hard. Many Rover managers and workers at Oxford remembered all too well the recurrent attempts by the Longbridge element inside the group to close Cowley. Woodley and his colleagues argued that, while rejection would have been fatal for Longbridge, it would also damage Solihull because BMW was considering making the next generation of Land Rovers in America. In the event, Woodley and the union leaders got their majority. The flexibility package was accepted.

However, Rover was by no means out of the woods. Goldman Sachs analysts said: 'We see how this system can help to produce a more efficient production system for the more successful plants within the Rover Group. Our fear remains that this might not be sufficient to offset the problems we see building at Longbridge.' The main concern was the time lag – possibly as long as five years – before BMW could replace the 200 and 400 models. Rover's rivals would not be standing still waiting for Rover to sort itself out. They saw Rover's ageing models as the soft underbelly of the British market and were prepared to attack them ruthlessly. Longbridge could bleed cash well into the next century. 'We still see the whole Rover venture as one that is fraught with risk,' said the Goldman analysts. 'BMW is discovering, as many others have, that taking a volume brand upmarket is not the easiest task to accomplish.' Pischetsrieder, however, remained determined and defiant:

> 66 BMW is among the most admired car manufacturers as a brand, entirely due to the fact that we stick to our guns. The biggest mistake you can make in our business is to be too short-sighted. You have to invest three to four years before a new product comes off the line. Then you have the product for six or seven years, and it takes time before you are earning any money from your investment. We are in a business where strategic decisions are often difficult to explain. But the tactical ones are always wrong 99.

Even under the huge storm clouds now lowering over Rover, Pischet-srieder still looked to the golden scenario that was fast receding into the distant horizon. To reach it, Rover needed top-class management, sustained and costly commitment from BMW, outstanding success with the 75 – and a lower pound.

Things had gone a long way – mostly downhill – since the high days of late summer 1996, when the freshly appointed Hasselkus had hosted a presentation to bankers at London's Festival Hall. 'I hope that, by the time I leave, Rover's success will have made it the focus of a Harvard Business School case study,' he said. Then he paused and added, with characteristically dry wit, 'Of course, if we fail I suppose we will also be the subject of a case study.'

That comment looked far less amusing in the cold light of early December 1998. While outside observers may have been impressed by the stoicism and resilience of Pischetsrieder and the nobility of Hasselkus's resignation, BMW's controlling shareholders, who had seen the value of their shares slide alarmingly, would have preferred ignobility and success. The Quandts' patience with the Rover experiment was beginning to wear thin. And no one was more alert to their growing restiveness than Wolfgang Reitzle.

PART FOUR

No return

CHAPTER 13

Every Man for Himself

WHEN WALTER HASSELKUS so nobly 'stood up to be counted', he stood up so publicly for two very good reasons. First, he believed it was the honourable thing to do. Second, it was a thinly veiled arrow aimed at Bernd Pischetsreider, the architect of the strategy Hasselkus had failed to deliver. Hasselkus believed, and rightly so, that he had been the sacrificial lamb offered to the stock markets in order to dampen their growing concerns over the continuing damage that Rover was inflicting on BMW's share value. Hasselkus's departure was designed to buy Pischetsreider time in order for him to put in place the three strands of his survival plan – £150m of wage related cuts (which the unions had virtually delivered), £1.2bn of investment in order to completely regenerate Longbridge (which the BMW supervisory board had agreed), and £200m of government aid.

By the time Hasselkus went, Pischetsreider believed that only the government leg of the treble needed to be delivered. Despite comments by Manfred Schoch that 'the position of the supervisory board was that we would stay in Longbridge as long as we got a reasonable amount from the British government', and that BMW needed the government aid to fund the Longbridge work, the reality was that the £200m BMW requested was, economically, a drop in the ocean. Symbolically, however, it had enormous significance. Pischetsreider said that the fact that Ford had received money for Jaguar to develop the S-type, the BMW 5-series rival, meant that BMW should receive similar aid. If it failed to materialize that would signal a reluctance on the government's part to support fully BMW's massive commitment. As Pischetsreider put it, 'If they didn't care, then why should we?'

Admittedly, the Ford grant had been given by the previous government, but by now it was clear that the government was also ready to provide financial support for Ford's plan to turn its Halewood factory into the plant that would make the baby Jaguar X400, which would compete with the 3-series. Pischetsreider thought that, as a matter of fairness and equal dealing, government aid should be forthcoming. He was, therefore, not best pleased when his initial requests were rudely rebuffed by Peter Mandelson, secretary of state for trade and industry. Mandelson said that Rover's future lay in the hands of the company.

Pischetsrieder and other BMW executives were exasperated by Mandelson's stance – so much so that they went public on their demand for fair treatment. They pointed out to anyone who would listen that Jaguar had received almost £72m from the previous Tory government towards the £400m project to build the new S-type at Castle Bromwich in Birmingham. That equated to almost 20 per cent of the overall project cost. BMW's own request for £200m for Longbridge was 12 per cent of the total investment. 'It is almost as if ministers and officials cannot bring themselves to believe BMW is in earnest and that, if the necessary money is not forthcoming, it will close,' said one observer.

Pischets-rieder and other BMW executives were exasperated by Mandelson's stance – so much so that they went public on their demand for fair treatment

BMW's request posed big problems for the government which – despite Mandelson's attitude – knew it could not allow a black hole to open up in the heart of a sensitive political area. It was obvious that, given the employment implications of a closure and the benefits to be gained from the investment plan, the government would want to keep Longbridge going. However, a £200m package entailed, in absolute terms, by far the biggest chunk of regional assistance for the car industry handed out since Nissan received £125m for its Sunderland car factory almost 15 years earlier. For a government committed to avoiding accusations of old Labour-style profligacy with taxpayers' money, and a new trade and industry secretary determined not to be seen as a soft touch for aid applicants, this was a big mouthful to swallow.

Under new Labour, large dollops of central government cash had been provided only in the form of loans (albeit long-term ones) – as in the case of Rolls-Royce, which got £200m for its Trent engine, or BAe which received £125m in loans to fund new Airbus aircraft, but only after the DTI had approved the sum, the Treasury had rejected it and Blair had brokered a compromise that gave BAe most of what it wanted but saved everybody's face.

The good offices of the prime minister, who began to keep a close eye on the Longbridge situation, were needed for a similarly happy compromise to be reached. That would only happen if the government recognized that BMW was not playing games. 'This is an unusual case in terms of applications for grant aid because BMW is not trying to blackmail the government,' said an analyst at the time. 'Support on the scale they have asked for is an absolute necessity because of the amount they themselves are already putting in.' More cynical observers believed a more profound force was at work behind the concern of an image-conscious government and newly promoted ministers keen to be seen to be driving a hard bargain.

'I think the government may genuinely be viewing this from the wrong end of the telescope,' said a motor-industry insider: 'When they look at Longbridge, all they see is the British car industry's basket case, always in the news for the wrong reasons. They wonder why they should be offering more than the absolute minimum and worry that they may just be throwing good money after bad. But they don't realize what's at stake here in terms of investment levels. They don't understand what £1.7 billion can buy you.' By that he meant that only with BMW's money could Longbridge have any kind of a future.

No sooner had BMW started to put public pressure on Mandelson than he was forced to resign, the week before Christmas 1998, over the house loan issue involving Geoffrey Robinson. Mandelson's replacement was the bespectacled former polytechnic lecturer, Stephen Byers, who had been a junior Treasury minister. Untried at this level, Byers was immediately thrust into the pressure cooker that is inevitable when politics meets industrial relations. Rover quickly took Byers to Longbridge, where it showed him into a locked room to which access was tightly controlled. Inside stood a vision of the 95-year-old factory's future. It was a large model of what Herbert Austin's plant would look like if, and when, BMW invested £1.35bn to transform it and build R30 there.

Byers was impressed by Rover's blueprint for a twenty-first century Longbridge and the insight into BMW's design for change helped underpin his subsequent declarations of support for the plant. Byers was naturally keen to stamp his mark on the DTI and such a high profile issue provided ample opportunity. However, he was also acutely aware of the Treasury pressure to curb government spending. He was soon being pulled in both directions.

While Byers's accession to the top job at the DTI had been the result of an unexpected and externally generated resignation, the parallel manoeuvrings now taking place at the top of BMW were completely internally generated. One Rover executive characterized the period after Hasselkus's resignation as 'every man for himself'.

The anti-Pischetsrieder, anti-Rover, pro-Reitzle faction that had always existed in Munich now believed its hour had come. The anvil on which they believed they could break Pischetsrieder's strategy was the question of whether BMW should invest in Longbridge and the new medium car. By now, Reitzle was openly refusing to sanction that investment. An anti-Pischetsrieder campaign began to gather momentum, orchestrated by Reitzle's allies and not discouraged by Reitzle himself. Pischetsrieder retreated into a siege mode and sought to defend the strategy by which he would stand or fall. But in the early New Year of 1999, the Reitzle supporters' campaign became increasingly aggressive and increasingly public. It littered the pages of the German business media.

The power struggle between Pischetsrieder and Reitzle had become so fierce that it threatened to paralyse BMW's decision-making process. Perhaps more importantly it threatened to blemish the much cherished BMW image. It was that image, so jealously guarded by the Quandts, which had to be protected at all costs. For von Kuenheim and the Quandts, who prided themselves on the discretion with which BMW was run, the open war for control of BMW's management board was acutely uncomfortable. The situation could not be allowed to persist.

The extraordinary battle came to a head on Friday 5 February 1999 at a supervisory board meeting on the twenty-first floor of the Four Cylinder.

Even at the time of writing, almost two years after the event, the definitive story of what happened that day has not emerged. However, piecing together the various strands of the story reveals a dramatic sequence of events.

Pischetsrieder arrived at 7 am on a gloomy Munich morning. As soon as the meeting began, two hours later, he formally tendered his resignation. It was quickly accepted by von Kuenheim, the man who had made him king six years earlier. Perhaps the alacrity of this reaction surprised the BMW chief, and some observers believed that, if Pischetsrieder had stood his ground and fought, he might have retained his job. But he had come to the conclusion that he had become a lame duck leader, and von Kuenheim was not in the mood to argue with him. A general discussion about whether to continue the multi-brand strategy ensued and the board then broke for lunch. All now seemed clear for Reitzle to inherit the crown.

Reitzle was insistent that BMW must pull out of Rover cars, but whether this determination played a part in what followed during the afternoon remains unclear. According to very reliable sources, von Kuenheim, having waved goodbye to Pischetsrieder, was equally determined that Reitzle should not take over. Whether he felt a residual commitment to the Rover strategy, whether he blamed Reitzle for the agonizingly public boardroom bust-up, or whether he simply believed he was the wrong man for the job, the veteran supervisory board chairman and custodian of the Quandts' special relationship with the company pulled the strings that hung Reitzle's chances. The afternoon resumption of the board meeting shattered his dream once more. As Tony Woodley put it, 'Reitzle played the big game twice – and lost, twice.' Reitzle, too, now resigned.

Von Kuhnheim also had the backing of a works council antagonistic towards Reitzle. Sources close to the supervisory board are adamant that Manfred Schoch refused to back Reitzle, even when it was obvious that Pischetsreider had lost the stomach for the fight. There was a kind of union solidarity at work. Indeed, it was the rupture of that solidarity a year later, amid rising fears in Germany that BMW jobs were being threatened by Rover's huge losses, that removed the last obstacle to dumping Rover.

Woodley admitted that the unions 'were disappointed and concerned at the removal of Pischetsreider, who they saw as their best hope for survival at Longbridge'. As he stated in an interview with Joy Batchelor of Warwick Business School, 'There's no disputing the fact that the effort between both countries to keep Pischetsreider in power and keep the Longbridge plan alive was the joint aim and objective.'

'Reitzle played the big game twice – and lost, twice.' Reitzle, too, now resigned

Whatever the precise details, the result was that the John Major syndrome was revisited. When two huge egos collide, a quiet man is often seen as the only viable alternative. Von Kuenheim and his colleagues therefore settled on their own John Major look-alike to steady the boat. At 7 pm that night, after hours of rumours and counter-rumours about the outcome of the meeting, BMW announced that both Pischetsrieder and Reitzle had resigned and that Joachim Milberg was the new chairman of BMW's management board.

CHAPTER **14** **Last Chance Saloon**

MILBERG, A 56-YEAR-OLD FORMER PROFESSOR of engineering at Munich's technical university, had joined BMW in 1993. At the university he had been a respected advisor to virtually every leading car company in the world. During his time at BMW he had been instrumental in creating one of the most efficient car plants in the world, at the company's manufacturing base in Regensburg, as well as being closely involved in the development of the Spartanburg plant in South Carolina.

Naturally there were concerns that Milberg would be too product oriented and perhaps too academic in his approach to the ever-increasing difficulties at Rover. Milberg took over a parent company and subsidiary in deep crisis. The board meeting which appointed him also approved the new Mini, which was to be built at Longbridge, and gave the go-ahead to facelifts for the 200 and 400 models.

However, the board stalled on approval for the replacement for the two models. That decision would be taken, in conjunction with Milberg, after he had carried out an audit of Rover. Milberg, Werner Samann, Rover's new chairman, and various colleagues met in Munich the weekend after the boardroom carnage and agreed to a complete review of BMW's operations worldwide. However, the real focus was on Rover, where Milberg and colleagues had to decide whether they could cut its huge losses and stick with Pischetsrieder's strategy of replacing the Rover 200 and 400 with the R30. They were faced with choices which included badging the new car as a Rover or Triumph, or reverting to Reitzle's concept of a BMW 2-series and building it at Longbridge.

More fundamentally, Milberg wanted a review of the strategy for expanding Rover as a parallel premium brand in the smaller car segment.

Notwithstanding the review, Milberg later told the company magazine, 'It has been, and remains, our clear-cut strategy to ensure the company's long-term independence and autonomy.' He and his team rapidly came to the same conclusion as Pischetsrieder had done six years earlier: that if BMW was to avoid being squeezed by the global giants into an ever-smaller and less profitable niche, it had to increase its volumes to around 1.8m units through Rover's presence in smaller cars. Only by so doing, BMW believed, could it sustain the virtuous circle it had painstakingly established over the past three decades: high margins that generate the cash needed for heavy investment in leading edge technology in order to create a product that in turn sustains the integrity of the BMW brand.

Like Pischetsrieder, who had recruited him, Milberg took the view that a BMW 2-series would dilute the exclusivity of the blue and white roundel. 'We need to have the entire product range from small car to Rolls-Royce, which will be produced under our direction as of 2003,' he said. 'You simply can't do that with a single brand. People want to be recognized as individuals – they don't want to be swallowed up into a standard-brand mass. When it comes to expressing one's individuality, the car is a crucial factor. And that is the key reason why the BMW brand is so successful.

'Why put that at risk?' Milberg asked. 'A multi-brand strategy allows us to focus sharply on the different segments.' Once the continuation of the Pischetsrieder strategy had been confirmed, Milberg moved rationally and relentlessly to try and ensure it paid off. He and his team, among whom Carl-Peter Forster, by then manufacturing supremo, was seen as his heir apparent, jettisoned the hands-off approach Pischetstrieder had adopted until near the end of his tenure.

Milberg ensured that Rover was rapidly absorbed into the BMW organizational framework to the extent that the British company's status as a distinct entity was scrapped. Rover Group, the reincarnation of British Leyland (BL) sold first to British Aerospace and then BMW, no longer existed. All functions, from engineering to sales and marketing, had finally been unified under the BMW Group banner. According to one car magazine, BMW had even chartered two Avro jets and one Airbus to fly planeloads of managers from Munich to Rover's Midlands operations on a daily basis. Those managers made up 'purge teams' that crawled all over

Rover to eliminate obstacles to the integration as well as reducing costs where possible.

The purge tag was particularly appropriate because the whole absorption process triggered an exodus of Rover managers and staff. Managers from Munich, therefore, controlled every aspect of the operation, from Samann down. It was said by Rover watchers that the newcomers showed open disdain for the management style and systems they found. This was culture clash Mark II, with the gloves off and without the sensitivity. The overall effect was to create a cultural revolution. Like other such movements, it created both huge change and considerable damage to the fabric of the business – not its bricks and mortar, in which BMW was investing vast sums, but its flesh and blood. One insider said bluntly: 'Basically, it's a human-relations disaster.'

> **The overall effect was to create a cultural revolution**

The alternative view was that Rover's management actually needed firmer direction. It seemed to some that BMW had veered from one extreme to the other and in the process thrown out the baby – or at least its feel for the British market and the marque – with the bathwater. 'They haven't listened to the Rover managers who knew a lot of the solutions to Rover's problems, but didn't know how to implement them or lacked the resources to do so,' said one analyst. 'The BMW people believe their processes will work here because they work in Germany,' he said. 'In the end, they are probably right, but the cost in terms of both money and organizational disruption will be enormous.'

Fortunately, the ructions did not spill over into disputes among Rover's workforce – which by that stage was heading towards 28,000, down from 39,000 in 1998. The reason was simple: the workers understood, more acutely than anyone else, that BMW was Rover cars' last chance. However, the weak launch of the 75 in Britain suggested that the changes made by BMW to Rover's sales and marketing personnel, now headed by a former BMW sales executive from Germany, were not solving the problem.

The £18,000 entry-level models, which may have attracted new British customers, were in short supply. Inadvertently, BMW had repeated the mistake made by BL 13 years earlier, when it launched the original Rover

800 in versions whose high prices discouraged buyers. The British sales problems need not necessarily have been fatal to the 75 because of the high proportion of its output aimed at continental buyers. But in the largest single market for the car, BMW's mistakes meant the 75 fell well short of target sales.

With sales failing to take off and pressure growing on car prices in Britain, BMW could only square the vicious circle in which Rover had become mired by cutting its costs. That meant, above all, forcing through price cuts from its predominantly British supplier base. 'BMW's problem is that it has a complete imbalance on the supply side,' said the analyst. 'While about 70 per cent of all new models are for export, about 70 per cent of the supply base is still in Britain.'

Euroland was Rover's main export zone. The buoyancy of the pound against the euro forced BMW into an attempt, unprecedented even in the price-conscious car industry, to slash procurement costs. It was already running two cost-cutting programmes: a supplier reduction scheme trading off higher volumes for lower unit prices and a 'compete programme' enforcing double-digit reductions in supplier returns on sales and assets. It had also told its big suppliers that it wanted them to invoice Rover in euros at a rate of 1.319 to the pound – an effective price cut of almost 19 per cent at the prevailing exchange rate of 1.60.

The exchange rate problem for the group was, however, less than it seemed, because the profitability of BMW sales in Britain – which had beaten the 70,000 mark the previous year for the first time – was being simultaneously boosted by the low euro. But for Rover it would take time for the cost benefits to flow through, and time was not on its side.

However, Milberg retained the cornerstone of BMW's revival plan for Rover – the £1.35bn project to build R30 at a redeveloped Longbridge. Milberg received board approval for the R30 and made clear how crucial the model was for group strategy. BMW cars held worldwide market shares of between 25 per cent and 30 per cent, whereas, 'When it comes to the Rover 200 to 400 models, we currently have a share of just 3 per cent', he said. 'That's where we need to ensure greater growth in the future. And that is why it's strategically essential for the BMW Group to be pre-eminently represented here with an outstanding product and to share in the market growth.'

However, throughout the British car industry, there was considerable doubt whether the R30, facing intense competition from cars such as Volkswagen's Golf, GM's Astra and Ford's Focus, could sell in sufficient volumes at high enough prices to justify BMW's huge financial commitment to the project. Prophetically, one big components supplier said: 'R30 and the new Mini [to be launched late that year as a stand-alone brand] will not be enough to pull Rover out of its problems. They will be too little, too late.'

Where's the Aid?

Running concurrently with Milberg's frantic attempts to turn Rover around were the continued efforts by BMW to obtain aid from the British government. On 3 March less than a month after taking over following the boardroom bloodbath, the newly ensconced Milberg went once again to the equally new Secretary of State, Byers, and made formal application for regional selective assistance (RSA). BMW was still looking for around £200m in aid and confidently expected little resistance. In fact, Byers initially made all the right noises. So much so that a BMW supervisory board scheduled for Thursday 18 March 1999 had the formal acceptance of a £180m offer on its agenda. However, 48 hours before that meeting, alarm bells began ringing at Rover. The T&G and other unions, their antennae honed by recent experience, quickly picked up signals that something was wrong.

Byers had played things by the book. The scale of the government aid package would be determined by three factors, he said: BMW's total investment, a big productivity improvement and a serious commitment to training and education. If, Byers implied, those elements met government criteria, a respectable offer would be forthcoming. Wires hummed between Whitehall, Warwick and Bavaria. The DTI's Industrial Development Advisory Board, which scrutinizes aid applications, met on 12 March to finalize its proposal. The board, chaired by Sir Anthony Cleaver, former head of IBM UK, is believed to have recommended the government offer of almost £200m towards the Longbridge overhaul, more or less exactly what BMW had offered.

This conclusion was informally communicated to Rover and BMW. The reaction at Rover was a collective sigh of relief. The company had endured a grisly seven months, with soaring losses, sweeping job cuts, a swathe of top management departures and, above all, the shadow over Longbridge. Now, at last, people could see light at the end of the long, dark tunnel. Then came a shattering revelation. The light they could see belonged to an express train driven by Byers, with his good friend Alan Milburn, Treasury chief secretary, on the footplate.

The light they could see belonged to an express train driven by Byers, with his good friend Alan Milburn, Treasury chief secretary, on the footplate

On the Monday evening before the BMW board meeting, Woodley fired off a warning shot: 'We hope the government does not misjudge the situation – £100m would be regarded as a derisory offer,' he told the *Birmingham Post*. By then, he knew that £100m was precisely the kind of figure the Treasury and the DTI were discussing. The difference between £100m and £180m was, in the context of BMW's already stated commitment, minute: its symbolic significance was, however, huge.

Far from going through with a £200m package, Byers – who was himself chief secretary before replacing Peter Mandelson at the DTI in December – had slashed it to £118m and phased it over five years. The proposal 'breaks new ground for a package of this nature', he said, without revealing details. Turmoil ensued inside Rover. At BMW, Milberg and his colleagues were shocked, all the more because their expectations of British support had been raised only to be dashed. On Thursday, the fifth anniversary of BMW's purchase of Rover from British Aerospace, its supervisory board met, so it thought, to accept a £200m offer. It turned out they were there to discuss a £118m reality.

The board announced that Rover's losses last year soared from £91m in 1997 to £650m. It was the company's worst result since its then chairman, Sir Graham Day, threw everything, including the kitchen sink, into the 1986 accounts and unveiled a bottom-line loss of £892m. With no relief from the high pound, which was crippling its export profitability and exposing its home market share to imports, Rover was likely to lose another £350m that year, according to analysts. BMW restricted itself to a gnomic comment about the aid negotiations: 'Given the current stage of discussions with the British government, the BMW board has not yet decided on the investment site for production of the successor to the Rover 200 and 400 series, it said.

What BMW did not reveal was that its directors had been infuriated by the government offer on Longbridge, both in its size and its conditions such as the long-term phasing of payments. Many of them already blamed the government, however unjustly, for driving up the value of the pound – the factor that, more than anything, is responsible for the huge losses made by Rover. To the BMW board, the government offer added insult to injury. BMW had invested £2.5bn in Rover in five years and planned to inject another £1.5bn of its own cash over the next three, making a total of £4bn. That would be more money in eight years than successive British governments provided for the company over two decades.

Privately, BMW executives made it clear to the DTI that, unless a much better offer were forthcoming, BMW's Longbridge plan would be unviable. The plant would close, with devastating consequences for the West Midlands, in particular, and for British industry in general. If that happened, a golden scenario – the last chance to reverse 30 years of decline in mainstream carmaking by Rover and its antecedents, BL and British Leyland – would be lost. Woodley said bluntly: 'The government is fiddling while Rome burns.'

More than any single protagonist in the Rover saga, Woodley had consistently recognized the scale of the Longbridge crisis. 'I have been worried from the beginning that we could lose this plant by mistake,' he said on Friday. 'I believe the government is under-estimating the attitude and expectations of BMW and I am very concerned now that we will not move forward far enough or fast enough.' Other observers were equally bemused. Julie Kirkbride, the Conservative MP for Bromsgrove, jumped on the emotional bandwagon when she said, 'I was absolutely stunned when I heard that BMW had been given [only] £118m for Longbridge. It seemed astonishingly cavalier; it seems as if they [the government] are playing poker with 50,000 jobs.' Tony Lancelott, engineering analyst at the Birmingham stockbroker Albert E Sharp, said: 'You cannot imagine the German or French governments allowing a big car factory to close.

Given the number of jobs that depend on such an operation, they would do whatever was necessary to secure its future.'

The next day, news began to filter through that the government might be prepared to raise its offer. Number 10 Downing Street began to exert pressure on Byers to sort out the mess. He duly told the Birmingham Chamber of Commerce annual dinner on Friday that he was committed to securing Longbridge's future. Byers said: 'I want to give you a personal commitment that I will discharge my duties to the employees of Longbridge and to the community.' Tony Blair was determined to avoid a return to old-style, across-the-board industrial subsidies, but he was also concerned that the government should give BMW every chance to succeed with its ambitious Longbridge reconstruction.

At the DTI, it finally dawned on ministers and officials that, as Woodley had always said, BMW was not playing games, but was in deadly earnest. However, there was still some work to be done on the detail and that was being held up, so BMW believed, by the government. A campaign of press innuendo was in full flow with Milberg stating at BMWs annual press conference: 'The longer the negotiations drag on, the greater will become the likelihood of a production site outside of Great Britain.'

This placed Byers in a dilemma. Nobody believed that the alternative, building a plant in Tatabanya, Hungary, was serious, but Byers could not say as much because such a statement would have further alienated the European Commission, which had to approve the Longbridge aid package. Comments from the Hungarian ministry of economic affairs to the effect that it knew nothing of any plans by BMW did not help matters. The truth about Hungary was that it had, indeed, once been considered by BMW and feasibility studies had been prepared. What happened with the RSA grant application was that BMW simply dusted off the old proposals and injected them into the negotiations. There was never any real chance of building Rovers in Hungary. As one highly placed BMW insider said: 'The only alternative to Longbridge is closing Rover cars completely.'

Byers was being squeezed by Number 10, the media, BMW, Rover and the unions. The day after Milberg's comments, Byers called him in Munich and said they could do a deal at around the £150m mark. The sum was to be made up of £129m in RSA, plus other amounts from some rates relief from Birmingham City Council and Advantage West

Midlands, the Skills Development Fund of the Regional Development Agency. Everybody was happy – or so it seemed. It was three months later before the deal was formally announced. In a 23 June 1999 press release entitled 'Rover deal heralds new approach to State aid for industry', Byers joyously announced:

> 66 This is great news for Longbridge, the West Midlands and the country as a whole. The Government looks forward to working with BMW to ensure the success of Longbridge and all its car plants in the United Kingdom. BMW's application for financial assistance is the first major application for government support that I have had to consider as Secretary of State. I was not prepared to deal with this in the traditional way by simply making a substantial payment to BMW. Instead I wanted the Longbridge agreement to be one which heralded a new approach to government assistance to industry – a new approach which reflects a long term commitment and not a quick fix. This is why I sought guarantees on productivity targets, raising skills and substantial investment from the company itself. Guarantees have been given in all these key areas. Because we were breaking new ground the negotiations were, of necessity, complex and detailed. I thank BMW for the constructive way in which they have conducted themselves throughout these discussions. The phasing of the £129m RSA over six instalments is essential in order to link financial support to productivity targets, and the bulk of the support will come in the final three instalments (£30 million in 2002; £26 million in 2003; £26 million in 2004). This will give time for the investment in improving skills and the development of the new plant to take place. This deal shows the way forward. A new approach fit for the century ahead. A new approach which safeguards tens of thousands of jobs but in doing so recognizes that for those jobs to be secure in the long term they need to be based on investment, productivity and skills. The workforce at Longbridge, BMW and the Government have all shown commitment to this project. The future is an exciting one, and I look forward to Longbridge taking on its competitors, winning and becoming a world leader 99 .

What he omitted to add in his self-congratulatory missive was that he had failed to clear the ground for the aid with the European Commission. The failure to do so would come back to haunt him.

Along with the formal DTI press release, BMW were also making contented noises at a deal well done. Milberg committed Rover to launching a new range of vehicles over the following five years including the mid-size models being manufactured at Longbridge. In total BMW had committed £1.5bn to Longbridge, a sum which illustrates the tokenism of the government's contribution. That £1.5bn was less than half the total earmarked for Rover which was to cover the launch of the new Mini as well as new Land Rover models. Milberg also announced new productivity pledges by the unions and even went as far as predicting that Britain would eventually join the European Monetary Union and adopt the single currency which would mean that sterling would no longer be an issue. All this occurred on 24 June, the day after Byers's official announcement. On that same day BMW's shares closed nearly 3 per cent down. It was clear that the euphoria exhibited by Byers and Milberg was not shared by the hard-nosed analysts on the Frankfurt exchange.

It was clear that the euphoria exhibited by Byers and Milberg was not shared by the hard-nosed analysts on the Frankfurt exchange

They knew that Rover was likely to clock up operating losses of more than £330m in the first six months of 1999 – almost as much as it lost at the operating level in the whole of 1998. European motor industry analysts said the grisly figures were being caused by a drive to clean out huge stocks of Rover 200 and 400 models before the launch of revamped cars later in the year. Keith Hayes of Goldman Sachs projected an operating deficit of at least DM1bn for Rover in the first half, and other analysts' forecasts were in a similar vein. Executives at BMW were determined to clear the way for the re-engineered, mid-range models, to be badged Rover 25 and 45. If those were to hold their initial prices, the overhang of their predecessor models had to be removed. But the marketing costs were proving astronomical.

The losses triggered fears of further job cuts at Rover, where almost 4000 jobs had been shed through voluntary redundancy in the previous six months. The workforce was already down to about 31,500, and experts predicted that, over time, it would fall by a further 5000. BMW was hoping for a sharp fall in second-half losses as cost savings came through and sales were boosted by the launch of the new upmarket 75 model.

Rover lost £647m before tax in 1998, but almost half that figure was related to extraordinary charges, including provision for the voluntary redundancies. Its operating loss was £466m, 70 per cent of which was incurred in the second half of the year. About £133m of that was related to the cost of extricating Rover from the short-term, fleet-rental market. Rover's main headaches were still the 200 and 400, which BMW inherited when it originally bought the company. The 400 was widely criticized from the outset for being undersized and overpriced. The 200 was better positioned but suffered in Britain from having to straddle both the supermini and lower medium market segments after Rover decided against developing a Metro replacement.

The 200 did well in continental European markets. But the profitability of those exports was destroyed by the surging pound. The models had been exposed in their home market to a flood of relatively cheap imports from Renault, Volkswagen and Fiat. Rover's British market share had fallen to an all-time low. In May the company took 5.89 per cent of the market compared with 9.42 per cent in May the previous year. In the first five months of 1999, Rover's overall British sales slumped by 29 per cent, compared with the corresponding period of 1998. The figures included Land Rover models, whose sales were actually surging. The current market share of Rover cars was estimated by experts at only about 3 per cent.

One big factor behind the unprecedented slump was that Rover had stopped production of the 100 (formerly the Metro) and the 800 executive saloon, and was running out of the 600 upper-medium saloon. Rover slashed sticker prices in March and Werner Samann, its new chairman, cut prices again, while also improving specifications in a bid to clear the backlog ahead of the planned autumn launch of the revised models. The price of the bottom-of-the-range 200 and 400 models was slashed by £1000. On the 200, equipment previously offered as optional, such as power steering and driver's airbag, was made standard. Price cuts of up to £1750 were also available on some 400 models. Such operating figures did little to allay the fears of those who still harboured fears that

Rover would somehow drag BMW down. It would not be very long before it was to emerge that, even if Milberg did not share those fears, the Quandt family certainly did.

15   **Escape to Alchemy?**

I N AUGUST 1999, Eric Walters, one of the founding partners of the private equity firm Alchemy, celebrated his birthday with a party at his house in Switzerland. One of the guests was his fellow Alchemy founder, Jon Moulton. There, surrounded by the soaring Alps, the two men fell to discussing what industrial peaks they might scale. They settled on something that, on the face of it, looked more forbidding than the Eiger and considerably higher than Mont Blanc. 'We were a bit short of large turnround targets,' Moulton recalled. 'But we agreed that the biggest in the UK was Rover parts. We thought that might be worth a shot.' The discussion was classic Moulton and Walters. Not for nothing had they chosen to name their firm after the process of turning base metal into gold. Alchemy was not your average, middle-of-the-road venture capitalist – as private equity firms used to be known even though most of them sought to minimize risk wherever possible. For the buccaneering Moulton, with a Merseyside accent that had defied a working life in the City, and the wiry, alert Walters, adventure was the name of the game: nothing ventured, nothing gained.

Although Alchemy was best known for its buyout of the Fads DIY paint chain, its founding partners had a heavyweight industrial pedigree and an appetite for operating at the edge. Their skill lay in recognizing how far they could go: it was a narrow margin, but Moulton and Walters had an acute sense of where risk became recklessness. Most private equity groups would have run a mile from Rover, in the unlikely event that the idea of buying it had ever occurred to them in the first place. Moulton and Walters were drawn to it like a magnet. The two men both had connections with Rover and the British motor industry. Walters was from

Coventry, where his grandfather had worked for the Standard Motor Company, one of the many groups subsequently consolidated into British Leyland.

Moulton had a more recent association with Rover. In 1988, while he was at Schroder Ventures, he had worked with Sir Graham Day on a buyout bid for Rover. The bid was well advanced when Lord Young agreed to sell the group to British Aerospace. 'We got to know quite a lot of the people in the motor industry, and became something of an expert on the industry, which suffers from a bit of a shortage of private equity deals,' said Moulton. Also part of the Alchemy team was Kevin Morley, who had been Rover's managing director for a period during George Simpson's leadership and who had set up his own marketing firm to handle the Rover advertising account before selling the company. Morley knew Rover inside out.

Moulton and Walters also had an entrée to BMW that meant they would not be merely cold calling. After Alchemy was founded in the early 1990s, they had identified the German market – where private equity activity was virtually unknown – as potentially fertile ground for buyout and buyin activity. They therefore established a German advisory board chaired by Tomas Sommerlatte, the former head of the management consultant Arthur D. Little. Sommerletter was noted for two factors, one personal, the other professional. On the personal front he was the proud father of 11 children. On the professional he had contacts throughout German industry. 'He knew everyone,' said Walters.

They were therefore intrigued when a message came back from Munich: BMW would be interested in a meeting

Among Sommerletter's acquaintances were the Quandt family and Eberhard von Kuenheim. Despite his retirement the previous May as supervisory board chairman, von Kuenheim was still very much in touch with events, while Stefan Quandt had become a deputy chairman of the company. 'I will have a word with them,' he told Moulton and Walters. Even with the German connection, Moulton and Walters thought their approach was the longest of long shots. They were therefore intrigued when a message came back from Munich: BMW would be interested in a meeting.

The lunchtime encounter took place in October over sandwiches on the twenty-second and top floor of the Four Cylinder. Moulton and Walters were welcomed by Helmut Panke, BMW's finance director, and Hagen Luderitz. Moulton and Walters did not make a proposal. They merely asked about BMW's intentions towards Rover. Luderitz replied with the strategy that had motivated the Rover takeover: BMW needed another brand to provide critical mass. To the Germans' surprise, Moulton criticized the strategy. BMW did not need Rover, which was the wrong brand for what BMW had in mind, he said. Why dilute BMW's outstanding name for sporty saloons asked Moulton, rhetorically. 'I gave him quite a hard time,' Moulton recalled.

It became apparent that one big factor behind BMW's desire for a smaller car range was the forthcoming environmental regulations that would penalize car companies with high carbon dioxide emissions. Moulton thought that was partly why BMW was so keen on the new Mini, because it would average down the CO_2 emissions from the model range. To the Alchemy duo, however, the most revealing response of all was from Panke. Luderitz did almost all the talking during the 90-minute meeting, declaring that BMW would carry through its agreed strategy – i.e. build Rover into a premium brand. At that point, Panke sat silent, his arms folded, staring across the table at Moulton and almost imperceptibly shaking his head. 'I thought, "We might just have a deal on here",' said Moulton later.

Even so, when the Alchemy board sat down the following Monday for its regular start-of-week review meeting, Moulton, Walters and co. put the chances of the Rover prospect materializing at about 0.2 per cent. They soon raised that estimate. Shortly after the first meeting, BMW came back with a request for a further discussion. 'We started to do some serious reading,' said Moulton. He and Walters called in Paul Bridges, one of their younger team members, and scoured every source for data on Rover. 'We had reams and reams of the stuff,' said Moulton. 'It became pretty clear what BMW had to do, and that was not to continue wasting money on Rover cars.'

The second meeting was also with Panke and Luderitz – indeed, throughout the negotiations, Moulton and Walters had little contact with anyone else from the BMW board. Amazingly, they never even spoke to

Milberg. BMW's executive chairman distanced himself from the whole discussion. At that second meeting, Moulton said, 'We moved into heavy duty.' This time there was no repetition of the talk about BMW needing a mass brand. 'That first meeting was the last time we heard that,' Moulton said. As they settled into their analysis of Rover and BMW, Moulton and Walters realized their timing had been spot on. 'We had got to it at the time they were just changing their minds,' Moulton said. He and Walters also knew the reason why: after studying all the numbers they could amass, they realized Rover was losing bucket loads of money.

BMW had also been losing heavily on its joint venture with Rolls-Royce in small aero-engines. But Milberg had at least partly resolved that problem by agreeing to swap BMW's 51 per cent stake in the joint company for a 10 per cent stake in Rolls-Royce plc. Once upon a time, when Eberhard von Kuenheim and Sir Ralph Robins had been mulling over such possibilities, this move might have been seen as the prelude to a merger of BMW and Rolls. But now analysts agreed it was an elegant way of positioning BMW to extricate itself from the costly aero-engine business. The group had a more liquid investment which could be cashed in at some point in the future, even if it was subject to the volatile performance of Rolls shares.

The aero-engine deal still left the much greater cash drain of Rover. Alchemy's partners reckoned they had a more precise idea of what Rover was costing BMW than BMW did. 'We told them what their losses for the year would be to within a few million,' Moulton said. 'Rover was going to lose about £600m cash.' That figure, virtually unchanged from the awful 1998 result, was almost the last straw for Milberg and Panke. The 75 had barely reached the European market, the revamped 25 and 45 had not been launched and the benefits of the productivity agreement and job cuts had yet to kick in. But from the moment it became clear that Rover's 1999 losses were not falling, the decision-making balance at the Four Cylinder started to shift from keeping Rover if possible to selling it if the deal was right.

At the moment Moulton delivered his losses forecast, many analysts were anticipating a Rover revival. Stephen Reitman of Merrill Lynch headlined a note on BMW published in August: 'Turning point at Rover'. Although Reitman predicted only a slight decline in year-on-year losses in

1999, he said the situation should then recover markedly. 'Year-on-year losses and sentiment should improve from now on,' he wrote. He quoted one BMW manager as saying: 'It feels at last that we are coming out of the swamp.' BMW had said: 'The [Rover] restructuring measures undertaken in the first half combined with the deliveries of new Rover 75, lead to expectations of a significantly improved result in the second half.' BMW's official stance, as stated by Milberg, was that Rover would halve its reported losses in 2000 and halve them again in 2001, before breaking even in 2002 – two years later than Pischetsrieder's original 1994 forecast.

But Alchemy's analysis, delivered by Moulton and Walters to Panke and Luderitz, differed strongly. Their message was that Rover would not meet Milberg's targets, because its losses could not possibly fall as far and as fast as he had suggested. BMW should therefore exit asap – and, of course, its best exit would be through selling Rover Cars to Alchemy. Moulton and Walters also had a piece of advice for BMW. Moulton said: 'We told them that their strategy ought to be to sell Land Rover at the same time as Rover, so that the profit and cash for Land Rover would cover the Rover loss. We told them that they should get £1.5bn for Land Rover.'

This was too much even for Panke. 'They were a bit taken aback,' Moulton recalled. 'They said, "We really want to keep Land Rover". I said, "I don't believe you. You have just developed a four-wheel drive car of your own[the X5]".' Although X5 had been developed in line with Pischetsrieder's philosophy of overlapping product lines between the different brands, what the Alchemy duo had realized was that it could now effectively replace Land Rover in the BMW portfolio. In fact, that could be its only sensible rationale.

The pfennig had dropped for Walters during his winter skiing holiday in Davos: 'The place was usually crawling with Range Rovers and Discoverys – it was a Land Rover preserve. But this year, I saw three X5s. Then it hit me: BMW had made a substitute of their own.' That view was only confirmed by what Moulton discovered through other motor industry contacts about the attitude at Land Rover to X5: 'There was serious antagonism at Solihull about the vehicle. They began to wonder what BMW was doing.' The X5 highlighted the way the two sides of the group were operating as separate, even competing companies.

At the second meeting, for the first time, Moulton and Walters outlined their concept of ditching the Rover brand and turning the business into the MG car company – a specialist sportscar maker 'with maybe a few saloons'. Eventually, this evolved into a plan to make around 50,000 MG-badged cars a year – a far cry from Rover's current production of more than 200,000, and even further from the original BMW plan to make almost 500,000 Rovers a year. What had once been the British Leyland Motor Corporation, the world's fourth largest carmaker after America's big three, would be boiled down to a kind of super-Morgan or TVR.

MG, the Alchemy team believed, 'was the only brand that's worth having out of what's left there'. As a brand, they thought Rover was dead – Moulton personally believed it had been beyond redemption by 1994, when BMW bought the business. The MG plan represented the culmination of the decades of decline since the formation of British Leyland in 1968. Since then, the cars business had been recurrently rebranded in an effort to reverse its relentless underlying decline. All the other famous names – from Austin and Morris to Triumph and finally Rover – had fallen away. But for Alchemy, this was not a reductio ad absurdum: it was a simple recognition of hard commercial reality.

Under the Alchemy plan, Rover cars would be wound down 'over a few months to a few years – we don't know the answer', they told Panke and Luderitz. 'We need some money to do that; we don't know how much,' they said. The job losses would be heavy: initially, around 4000 of the assembly jobs at Longbridge would go – more than half the total employed on the production lines. The engine plant workforce was already destined to fall significantly, because Hams Hall would be a much more productive facility.

The BMW executives then agreed to provide Alchemy with some information to enable Moulton and Walters to progress their proposal. The whole thing had to be handled very delicately, in a way that would not alert Rover, although it was now being run entirely by BMW-installed managers. The situation was complicated by the fact that Rover group was a single entity, of which Land Rover was part. Only Luderitz, the great survivor, would have appreciated the fact, but the secrecy of the discussions and their restriction to a handful of participants was reminiscent of how it had all begun six years earlier, with BMW's clandestine courtship of Simpson and Lapthorne.

Before matters went further, Moulton and Walters believed, BMW checked the bona fides of the Alchemy team. 'They got references in the car trade, and they concluded that we seemed to be credible, that we took on tough cases,' Moulton said. A series of meetings ensued during November and early December at which the approach of Panke and Luderitz changed. According to Moulton and Walters: 'Their attitude with us was now like someone making a business case study: "what if we do this, or do that?" We talked through just about every combination you could reasonably imagine.'

Those scenarios ranged from Alchemy taking Rover cars in its entirety, including Mini, the 75, Cowley and the Longbridge transmission plant as well as Longbridge assembly with MGF and the renamed 25 and 45. Alchemy found the conversations difficult, because in most cases BMW could not provide all the information Moulton and Walters needed. Sales figures were provided, but they related more to Rover's five-year plan than to what was happening in the marketplace. Alchemy's efforts to compile a balance sheet for Rover were hampered by lack of precise and up-to-date financial information.

It gradually dawned on the Alchemy team that BMW in Munich had never gripped Rover and got to the heart of the business. 'Rover was silo-managed,' they said. 'The design department operated in one silo, the engineering guys in another, marketing in another.' For Moulton and Walters that explained a lot about what had gone wrong. But it also made problematic the task of putting together a detailed offer.

> **It gradually dawned on the Alchemy team that BMW in Munich had never gripped Rover and got to the heart of the business**

Publicly, Milberg was maintaining BMW's commitment to the dual brand strategy. He told the January issue of *BMW Magazine*, the publication for BMW owners: 'To spell it out, the Rover 200 to 400 models will have successors that will be built in Britain.' Milberg said that, while BMW models had world market shares of 25–30 per cent in their respective segments, in the 200/400 segment BMW had a share of only

3 per cent. 'That's where we need to ensure greater growth in the future,' he said. 'And that is why it's strategically essential for the BMW group to be pre-eminently represented here with an outstanding product and to share in the market growth.'

BMW wanted to cover the entire product range from small car to Rolls-Royce, he said. The only satisfactory way of doing that was a multibrand strategy: 'You simply can't do that with a single brand. People want to be recognized as individuals, they don't want to be swallowed up into a standard brand mass. When it comes to expressing one's individuality, the car is a crucial factor. And that is the key reason why the BMW brand is so extraordinarily successful. Why should we put that at risk? A multi-brand strategy allows us to focus sharply on the different segments.'

The strategic imperative was clear and categoric: 'We want to have a pre-eminent position in the lower segment with the Rover 200 and 400 models,' Milberg told his interviewer. 'Wait and see – we will bring about a renaissance of the Rover brand.' With hindsight, that interview resembled nothing so much as the repeated statements by British Aerospace executives, from the moment in 1992 when they decided to sell Rover until the day the BMW deal was done, that Rover was a core business.

In reality, BMW was now accelerating towards the disposal that would kill the multibrand strategy. Milberg later reported to shareholders: 'At the end of the year, it became clear that the general conditions for the Rover brand were deteriorating dramatically – the British pound climbed to over DM3. As a consequence of this, serious consideration was given to a strategic reorientation of the BMW group.' The first public sign that the intense debate underway in the BMW boardroom might have reached a terminal phase came in mid-January at the Detroit motor show. Henrich Heitmann, BMW's sales chief, told the Suddeutsche Zeitung that 2000 'must see the turn' at Rover. He added, ominously, that Rover would now need eight to ten years to re-establish itself fully in the world market. This was the bleakest prognosis yet. Then, in words loaded with foreboding – and forewarning – Heitmann added: 'I fear that we do not have the time that we need.'

Walters had spent Christmas in Davos while Moulton went to Barbados, but once they returned the pace of negotiations quickened. Six or eight meetings followed, with Panke and Luderitz asking Alchemy how it would manage the rundown of Longbridge to create the streamlined

MG company. That was something Alchemy had not decided, since it did not yet know precisely what was to be in the package: the 75 and its production line were in and out on different occasions. BMW did not have all its irons in the Alchemy fire. In parallel with the Moulton–Walters talks, Milberg was sounding out a series of carmakers to see whether they were interested in taking Rover.

One Saturday morning in early February 2000, Jac Nasser, Ford's chief executive, paid a secret visit to Longbridge. Nasser had approached BMW a year earlier, after the boardroom bloodbath, with the offer of an alliance. It was Ford's second attempt to forge a US–German union, because Alex Trotman, previously Ford's chairman, had made overtures to Schrempp at Daimler-Benz before the DaimlerChrysler deal. Nasser was told that a minority stake in BMW might be available if Ford was prepared to take over Rover. For the astute Ford boss, that price was too high. Ford was wallowing in over-capacity in Europe and, having effectively closed one British volume car plant by transferring Halewood to Jaguar, was beginning to plan the closure of its Dagenham factory.

Nasser needed two more British factories, especially the half-empty Longbridge, like a hole in the head. He politely declined BMW's invitation, issued a regretful statement that said 'BMW wishes to remain independent and I guess we have to respect that' – and recruited the newly departed Reitzle as head of the Premier Auto Group of upmarket brands that Ford was assembling. Nasser's whistlestop return to the Rover scene did not mean his attitude had changed. But he wanted to ensure that Ford should not miss out on the action if something fundamental was moving at BMW. In fact, as Nasser soon discovered, the terms on which BMW wanted to rid itself of Rover were even less alluring than the less than enticing criteria outlined by BMW the previous year.

Apart from Ford, BMW held serious talks about Rover with General Motors. It also notified VW and Toyota about its interest in selling out, while contacts also took place with Fiat. Some of them were not interested at all, while those that were wanted a significant minority stake in BMW as the quid pro quo. That, as Samann later revealed to the House of Commons trade and industry select committee, was non-negotiable. 'None was interested in buying the whole package,' Samann said of the other carmakers. 'The BMW company is not for sale. All negotiations regarding one single share in BMW were cancelled immediately.'

Moreover, BMW's need to find a solution to the Rover conundrum was becoming ever more pressing. By late February, it was apparent to Milberg and his management board colleagues that, far from improving, the Rover cars situation was if anything deteriorating. Contrary to earlier expectations of a year-on-year reduction in losses, Rover's total 1999 deficit, including redundancy costs, was £750m, up from £642m in 1998. In Britain, its market share had slumped during the year by more than two percentage points to 4.6 per cent – less than half the 11.3 per cent at which it stood when BMW bought the company. Rover car sales declined by 32 per cent during the year to less than 204,000, although that was partly due to the end of Rover 100 production at Longbridge and the changeover to the 75 at Cowley. Even Land Rover sales dipped slightly – the first annual decline for almost a decade.

BMW had no doubt about the villain of the piece. The pound, which had averaged DM2.48 in the first year of BMW's Rover ownership – and which had dropped to DM2.26 in the second year – climbed further. The pound had averaged DM2.97 in 1999, and by the year end was heading well beyond DM3. Milberg has always claimed that BMW warned the British government about the pound. He said, 'We pointed out that due to currency developments alone the BMW group was losing more than £1m with Rover every day, a loss clearly not acceptable and economically viable any more.' At that level, Rover was running as hard as it could on the productivity improvement and cost-cutting front – and still going backwards. 'We were losing £2,000 a car,' said one Rover manager. 'You couldn't possibly sell enough cars to compensate for the price cut that was necessary to make them competitive in the market.'

Far from gradually moving Rover up to premium pricing levels, the company was actually being forced to price down. The already distant prospect of rebuilding shattered margins was now so remote as to be virtually non-existent. Losses in 2000 were likely to be as high, if not higher, than in 1999. However, even at that stage Milberg was fiercely denying any change in strategy. In the January 2000 shareholders letter for the 1999 FY he stated that 'the Rover restructuring programme will continue to be vigorously pursued'. BMW continued with what amounted to a disinformation programme throughout the first quarter of

2000. For example, a letter to the Rover workforce, in the middle of February, said that 'BMW's commitment to Rover remains total'. At a sales conference later that month BMW assured dealers that BMW were not 'negotiating the sale of … any part of the business to anyone'. And yet, despite such protestations, Rover had acquired another nickname in Germany even more damning than the English Patient. They were calling it 'the bottomless pit' – the term by which every West German had long since learned to disparage East Germany.

BMW continued with what amounted to a disinformation programme throughout the first quarter of 2000

It was clear that Milberg's revised target of Rover breakeven in 2002 was now unattainable. That fact would become apparent when BMW reported its full-year results in March. There was a huge threat to the share price, which had slumped in the first half of 1999 on fears about Rover, but had since partially recovered on hopes of some kind of resolution to the problem. Even then, the shares stood 20 per cent below the peak they had hit in mid-1997 when Rover turnround optimism was at its zenith. BMW set enormous store by the annual shareholders' meeting, due in mid-May. Unless it could offer a way out of the Rover disaster by then, there would be hell to pay.

In fact, the issue was never likely to stay unresolved that long. It would be addressed on the supervisory board, by Stefan Quandt and his sister Susanne Klatten. The relationship between the Quandts and the board remained hidden from Alchemy's eyes, but Moulton said: 'We knew there were meetings, but we had no idea what was being said.' What Alchemy did know for certain was that, as Moulton said: 'Rover was killing them. It was haemorrhaging cash like crazy. They had no means of dealing with it.'

Despite the multibrand strategy and all the money that had been poured into Rover over six years – about £3.4bn, more than British governments had invested in BL in twice that timespan – BMW had only one road left for Rover: the exit route. And with the other carmakers uninterested in Rover alone, Alchemy was the only game in town. Milberg said later: 'It became very clear in the opening months of 2000 that a reversal of the trend [of Rover losses] was not to be expected. The Rover brand was further damaged because its future was increasingly called into question both in public and in the professional media. Above all in the United Kingdom, Rover's most important market, customers were responding with growing purchasing reticence. All this means that staying with Rover is no longer an acceptable business proposition.'

Milberg kept such thoughts to himself during the Geneva motor show, which began on 28 February. In fact, Carl-Peter Forster, BMW's manufacturing director, when specifically asked about the significance of the government aid for the R30, actually said that the 'project will go ahead irrespective of Brussels'. The truth had always been that in economic terms Brussels was always irrelevant. Many senior BMW managers were in the dark, although they had suspicions that something was cooking. On the BMW–Rover stand that Monday afternoon, one said: 'I meet people from the supervisory board and they smile and chat happily, but if you asked me what was really going on, I couldn't tell you.'

There were, however, an increasing number of straws in the wind. Carl-Peter Forster, dropped another, albeit contradictory, hint on the Monday evening in Geneva when he told journalists that, even if the European Commission approved the £152m aid package for Longbridge, BMW might not be able to justify proceeding with the plant and product investment. Two days later, a BMW spokesman said the group would have to rethink future investment in Rover if the pound continued to strengthen against the euro.

As he waded through the media crowds at Geneva, Milberg kept his thoughts to himself and his plans locked in his briefcase. Back in Britain, Samann was disinformative. At a meeting with Stephen Byers at the DTI, less than a month before the sale announcement, he clearly indicated that BMW's Rover strategy remained unchanged and that the company and the government should continue to progress the case in Brussels for the £152m aid package to be approved. Alan Clark, the former defence minister, had a phrase for Samann's approach. He called it 'being economical with the actualité'.

The actualité was that Panke and Luderitz were now moving fast towards an agreement with Alchemy. They knew that speed was of the essence. On Monday 6 March Moulton and Walters were called to a meeting at Munich airport. The negotiators did not even book a room at a nearby hotel. Instead, they sat down in the airport's business centre. The discussions now were about how Rover was to be carved up and, in particular, how the Longbridge site was to be divided. BMW had produced what Alchemy thought was an incredibly complex plan that resembled a patchwork quilt, with various pieces allocated to Alchemy – notably, of course, the car production lines – and others reserved by BMW, such as the engine and gearbox plant. But the map was not entirely accurate: 'One line went straight through the middle of the assembly hall,' said Moulton. Alchemy kept the map as a souvenir; it adorned a wall of the Covent Garden offices until being relegated to the Rover files.

At the airport meeting, the BMW side also asked Moulton and Walters roughly how much they would want to take Rover away. This was the key issue, because the money that would change hands in the deal would not be the purchase price: it would be the dowry BMW handed over to persuade Alchemy to take Rover on to its books. Moulton and Walters could not give a precise answer, because they were still unhappy with the level of financial data available. A week later, Moulton and Bridges flew to Munich again and headed for the Four Cylinder. The meeting was decisive. The two sides reached outline agreement on a deal under which Alchemy would take over Rover cars, including the 75 model (although not the Rover brand) which would be moved from Oxford to Longbridge. Rover would be renamed the MG Car Company, and Alchemy would buy Rover Group Ltd for £20m. But in return, BMW would pay Alchemy £500m, a sum designed to cover the cost of the drastic slim-down process and to provide some cash on top. Alchemy would get the cars Rover currently had stockpiled and the Longbridge plant for nothing. BMW was effectively giving Alchemy the Rover carmaking operation, except for Cowley.

Alchemy's own plan was to get the business in shape as MG, run it for up to three years, and sell it to a big carmaker or possibly float it. They also started serious talks with Lotus and, indeed, had one meeting with Proton. Alchemy insiders thought Volkswagen might well be interested, since it was building a specialist brands portfolio and had expressed interest in the past in having a British assembly base. Alchemy would have a six-week exclusivity period in which to conduct due diligence – the process of financial data discovery undertaken in all mergers and acquisitions. BMW agreed to pay Alchemy a fee if, after the due diligence was completed, the deal did not proceed.

The two sides were working towards the signature of a letter of intent. Then Panke told Moulton that the deal would be announced three days later, on Thursday. Moulton was amazed: 'It is very unusual to make a firm announcement on the back of a letter of intent,' he said. But BMW was in a hurry, as Walters quickly found out. 'I came back from a conference on the Monday, and was told: "You are in Munich tomorrow",' he said. His meeting was with Henrich Heitmann, the sales and marketing chief, and the subject was the sensitive matter of distribution. How, Heitmann asked Walters, did Alchemy plan to handle distribution? Walters said he had no idea. Everything depended on the contracts with distributors and dealers that Alchemy would examine during the six-week exclusivity period. Walters already knew the question was complicated, because of the intermingling in different countries of BMW, Rover and Land Rover dealerships.

Despite myriad unanswered questions, BMW was now on a crash course to the revelation that it planned to sell Rover cars. Rumours that it was preparing to pull out of Rover were now flying, fuelled by a Tuesday report in the *Suddeutsche Zeitung* to that effect. According to the report, which proved to be uncannily accurate and later triggered a German stock market inquiry into the consequent rise in BMW shares, the BMW supervisory board would make the decision on Thursday. The British government was alarmed. So were Woodley and the unions. Inside Rover, where even senior executives had been distanced from the Alchemy talks, a handful of people had learned the previous Friday that the company was to be sold. But they had no idea of the purchaser's identity.

BMW was now on a crash course to the revelation that it planned to sell Rover cars

The next day, Wednesday 15 March Moulton, Walters and Bridges arrived at 1 pm at the offices of BMW's London lawyers, Norton Rose, near Liverpool Street station. The wheel had come full circle: just over six years earlier, the same offices had been where Luderitz and Lapthorne had reached agreement on the Rover deal. The Alchemy negotiations lasted all night. At 6 o'clock on Thursday morning, the two sides finally signed the letter of intent. Hours later, BMW announced that it had reached agreement in principle to sell Rover cars and its Longbridge assembly operation to Alchemy. BMW would move production of the new Mini to Oxford, while Alchemy shifted the Rover 75 to Longbridge.

Instead of pursuing the multiple brand strategy, BMW now planned to develop its own sub-3-series car, christened the 2-series by the media, although BMW executives bridled at the name. One alternative being canvassed was Dixi, after the first car that BMW ever made. However, since that vehicle was derived from an Austin, the name may be considered inappropriate.

Instead of building the small car in Britain, as would have been the case if BMW had kept Rover, the company was surveying various sites across central and eastern Europe. Irony of ironies, although the Hungary option had started life as no more than a stalking horse and reference point to secure European Commission approval for the £152m Longbridge aid package, it had now become a reality. Slovenia, Poland and the Czech republic were also under consideration for the small car. So Reitzle, although he had lost his BMW job, had won the long argument over Rover cars. How far, of course, his running battle with Pischetsrieder had fatally delayed the Rover turnaround, and therefore turned his case against Rover into a self-fulfilling prophecy, was open to debate.

But there was no disputing the U-turn that Milberg had been forced to make from his statements only months before that the overlapping, multi-brand strategy, devised by Pischetsrieder, was the right one. The BMW chairman simply admitted that he had reversed his strategy. The lower priced segment of the market was now 'ripe' for a BMW, he said later. To the world at large, it was the end of the road for BMW's hugely expensive Rover experiment – or, as one headline put it: 'It's all Rover now'. Initially, most of the interest centred on Kevin Morley and the deal was presented as his comeback to Rover. But soon Alchemy decided that Morley's previous commercial relationship with Rover required that he should keep his head down, and Moulton himself emerged from the backroom to be the front man. One of his tasks was to find a chief executive who would actually run Rover for Alchemy.

BMW's announcement sent a shockwave through the West Midlands, where there was enormous concern about the implications for the regional economy of the huge cut in output envisaged by Alchemy. It was not only the manufacturing side, both in Rover and at its suppliers, that felt threatened.

Rover dealers were also faced with a precipitate reduction in throughput. A West Midlands task force was quickly constituted to examine the impact of the Longbridge sale, and how its worst effects could be mitigated. The task force was headed by Alec Stephenson, brother of Nick. Alec was a former head of Rover's powertrain operation and chairman of the West Midlands regional development agency, whose members included John Towers, who had headed Rover engineering under Hasselkus but had left after the Samann takeover and the total absorption of Rover into BMW.

Alchemy, meanwhile, was getting down to the task of completing its due diligence. In total, including advisers, Moulton and Walters now had 100 people working on the deal. In many respects, they were starting from scratch: 'At the time the deal was announced, we had never met anyone from Rover, we had not been to the Longbridge site, and had never had anything to do with the finance department, apart from very fragmentary contact.' According to Moulton and Walters, the Alchemy team soon discovered that many facts contained in the letter of intent were wrong. BMW executives had simply been unaware of the real situation at Rover. 'They were shocked by things our investigation found out,' said Moulton. 'The due diligence process was a mutual voyage of discovery.'

One of those on the BMW side who did not last the distance was Heitmann. Walters met him on the Friday morning, the day after the Alchemy sale announcement. While Walters wanted to cover the dealership position in each country, Heitmann was preoccupied with the German situation. There, BMW dealers had been encouraged by the promise of Rover sales growth to take on Rover franchises: now that promise would never materialize. Heitmann left the meeting with Walters – and resigned hours later. So did Forster and Wolfgang Ziebart, engineering supremo. All three had only joined the management board 13 months earlier, after the day of the long knives that resulted in the departures of Pischetsrieder and Reitzle. In the space of 14 months, because of the Rover issue, BMW had lost five of its top executives. Even for the motor industry, which has a colourful history of boardroom bust-ups, bloodletting on this scale was unprecedented.

The three had apparently gone because they disagreed with the other half of BMW's exit from Rover: the sale of Land Rover. Within 48 hours, it emerged that Ford was negotiating to buy the Solihull business for almost £2bn. That sum was almost identical to the Euro 3.15bn write-off that BMW said it would be taking on the Rover cars disposal. Milberg, Panke and Luderitz had taken Moulton's advice about how to exit Rover at nil net cost, at least in financial terms. It then emerged that Land Rover, far from being the profit machine that it once was, had lost almost £100m in 1999. Ford subsequently negotiated a slight reduction in the purchase price to £1.8bn, with about £500m of the payment deferred until 2005.

Apart from the three BMW directors, all parties seemed to be satisfied with the Land Rover sale, not least Reitzle, who – as chairman of the Premier Auto Group into which Jac Nasser slotted Land Rover – now inherited his own product plan. Milberg justified the Land Rover sale on the grounds that the X5 was proving an outstanding success, and that therefore 'a credible differentiation between the products offered by Land Rover and the X5 would have become increasingly difficult'.

Once again, there were echoes of the British Aerospace strategy that led to the Rover deal in the first place. Just as BAe had concentrated on stripping away all its underperforming businesses, notably Rover, so that the large profits of its defence arm could feed straight through into the group results, so BMW wanted to remove all drags on the BMW brand, which was going from strength to strength with demand at near-record levels and profits exceeding £1.3bn in 1999.

Milberg was now emphasizing BMW's ability to have a premium product in each market segment, topped and tailed by Rolls-Royce and Mini: 'Absolute size measured in production figures alone is not crucial to the success of the BMW group,' he wrote. 'In turnover per car, BMW ranks second worldwide [behind Porsche], far ahead of other carmakers.' Nonetheless, the Rover announcement triggered a spate of takeover rumours. One recurrent story was that BMW had already agreed to go in with Ford. In fact, the reverse was true. The terms of the Land Rover deal included a clause preventing Ford from making a bid for BMW for a year. The whole Rover withdrawal was designed to buy BMW's management a breathing space during which it could revive the share price. In this, the announcement that Panke had rushed to make achieved its aim: BMW's shares soared on the Alchemy news.

But while most outsiders now took it for granted that the Alchemy deal would go through, Moulton and Walters were making no such assumptions. For them, signing the letter of intent was only base camp. And the deeper they delved, the less they liked what they saw. 'There were distribution issues, warranty issues, tax issues and pension issues,' said Moulton. 'This was a business turning over £3 billion a year. Transactions don't get any more complicated.' Distribution, he said, 'was a total nightmare'. In France, where the three franchises – BMW, Land Rover and Rover – had been merged into one, the process of separating out Rover would be complex in the extreme. Alchemy believed it would also create employment and contractual law problems.

Similar difficulties cropped up around the world. In Australia, the dealers had five separate franchise arrangements; apart from the big three, there were also discrete Mini and MG franchises. Another issue was the value of Rover's unsold cars. New Zealand, one of the few right-hand drive markets in the world, was the last refuge for vehicles that were surplus to British and Japanese demand. The number of MGFs in New Zealand, according to Alchemy, was equivalent at prevailing rates of sale to 25 years' stock.

One of the main reasons for the overhang, Moulton said, was that dealers there had been told to price BMW's Z3 sports coupe at £3000 less than the MGF – another sign of how the BMW side of the group had competed against Rover instead of working with it. The worldwide stocks – but particularly those in Britain, where thousands of unsold cars were scattered across disused airfields – also formed by far the biggest element in Rover's asset base. 'We were going to get a £500m dowry and a balance sheet with a lot of assets that could be converted into cash,' said Moulton. But during the due diligence period, BMW sold many of the stockpiled cars at reduced prices, effectively liquidating many of the assets Alchemy had expected to acquire.

By the first week of April, with the halfway point in the exclusivity period approaching, Alchemy already knew it was going to have a long list of questions for BMW before it signed up to a deal. But by then, a rival attempt to take over Longbridge was underway. It had begun, just as the Alchemy move had started, with a piece of cold calling on BMW. About two months earlier, BMW had been approached by Lola, the specialist racing company owned by the multimillionaire Martin Birrane and run by David Bowes, who had worked for Alex Stephenson in Rover powertrain. Bowes' former colleague, Alex's brother Nick Stephenson, was a Lola non-executive director.

Lola wanted to buy the MG name from BMW. Bowes and Nick Stephenson got a dusty answer from Munich – then in the throes of setting up the Alchemy agreement – but they maintained their interest and kept a watching brief on Rover. In mid-March, when news of the impending Rover deal started to leak out, Bowes and Nick Stephenson contacted Alex at the development authority. They were just about to ask him to ring the Government to find out what was going on when, the day before the deal was announced, the Cabinet Office rang from Number 10, Downing Street to ask Alex Stephenson what he knew.

Lola wanted to buy the MG name from BMW

In the course of the inquiries that ensued, Jon Moulton's name surfaced. Then BMW made its stunning announcement, and the details of what Alchemy was being offered fell into place. 'It was plain that BMW was washing its hands of Rover,' said one person close to what became the Phoenix consortium. The discussion immediately turned to whether they could make a counter-offer. Also involved was Terry Whitmore, former plant manager at Cowley, who now ran the automotive division of the engineering design and manufacturing group Mayflower. Whitmore was therefore responsible for producing the MGF bodies under the Rover–Mayflower joint venture that BMW had left in place.

At around 8 pm one night the following week, Nick Stephenson was in his garden when his mobile phone rang. According to Phoenix, the caller was Jon Moulton, offering Stephenson the post of chief executive in the MG Car Company. However, Moulton tells a different story. Moulton says that while he was in conversation with Alex Stephenson, ostensibly in his role as head of the task force, Stephenson suggested that his brother, Nick, might be 'a good idea for the CEO'. Although Nick was on Alchemy's 'possibles' list, he was low on that list. Nevertheless, Moulton did ring Stephenson. Stephenson talked on for a while before admitting he was actually involved with a potential counter-bid. Moulton admits going berserk. He sent a 'rude fax' to the DTI demanding clarification of both the Stephensons' roles in the matter. The DTI officials said that, while they were not prepared to put anything in writing, they would instruct Nick Stephenson to phone Moulton and confirm he had no involvement with a rival consortium.

By 9 pm Stephenson's mobile was ringing again. This time, it was the DTI. The official begged Stephenson to back off for fear of jeopardising the Alchemy bid. Stephenson duly complied. Moulton took his call in the presence of a listening lawyer and claims Stephenson 'categorically denied any involvement' in a rival bid. Moulton remains angered by the incident to this day.

16 **Escape to Phoenix?**

S TEPHEN BYERS AND HIS DEPARTMENT were in a state of extreme agitation – a euphemism for near panic. It was little wonder, Byers had been personally lambasted for failing to see the Rover bombshell coming. His mitigation, that he had been badly misled by Samann, merely reinforced the view that he was severely out of his depth. Milberg's later account makes the point. As he told the *Sunday Times* in April 2000, 'Around the 20th [December 1999] I called Byers and told him that Rover was in critical survival mode – in serious trouble. The government, as well as the unions, should have known – how could they not have known – the true situation or Rover cars. We had given them regular figures of what was happening that left them in no doubt we were in a critical situation and had to find a solution. If we had kept on, we would have damaged BMW.'

Part of Byers' evidence to the House of Commons select committee inquiry was that 'one of the reasons I was so angry is the failure of BMW, six days before their supervisory board meeting to give any indication that the break up of Rover Group and the sale of Land Rover was even being considered'. If this truly was a surprise then either Byers's advisers fell down on the job in not pointing out the desperation of BMW's plight, or Byers did. What else did Byers expect? And why did he only ever talk to the BMW executives Milberg and Samann, instead of trying to get closer to the horse's mouth in the shape of the Quandts.

The select committee may have absolved Byers of 'misleading Parliament', but it failed to mention his inadequacy in understanding the business game in which he was engaged and his naiveté in playing that game. Byers's anger was the consequence of his surprise, which was self-induced; the evidence was there but he misread, or ignored, the signals. John Towers has said that Byers should not be so castigated. 'Who', he asked, 'in their right mind is going to put their political reputation on the line for this organization called the Phoenix Consortium at the last minute; who are said to not have any financial muscle; who claim, and rightly so, to have some expertise in the industry but are putting together a deal in a way that has never been attempted before? For a senior politician to stand up and support us in the way he did was a "bold move, Minister".'

Byers was not acting sensibly or rationally he was acting out of ignorance

Precisely. Byers was not acting sensibly or rationally, he was acting out of ignorance. In Towers' view Byers was 'ambushed' by BMW. People are ambushed because they are either arrogant or un-prepared (weak intelligence). Despite numerous attempts to speak with Byers, we were unable to secure an interview.

Whatever the reason for the DTI mistakes, one consequence of Byers's embarrassment at the situation in which he found himself, was for the trade and industry secretary to give a fulsome, and knee-jerk, reaction to the Alchemy bid. The DTI attitude was that anything was better than closure, the ultimate nightmare, and the Alchemy bid at least was something.

But those two calls to Stephenson, within an hour, had touched the mild-mannered businessman on the raw. He was genuinely affronted by the DTI plea and the Moulton call to the department that had sparked it off. Nonetheless, the inchoate team of Lola and Mayflower directors had acceded to the DTI and backed off. However, a few days later, the DTI attitude changed. One of the change agents may have been a meeting between Moulton and, on the other side, Woodley, for the unions, and Towers, for the task force. Accounts of this meeting differ. According to the Phoenix camp, Woodley was appalled by Moulton's detailed plans for more than halving the workforce. Moulton, by contrast, said: 'Tony Woodley and I met on numerous occasions during the deal and we never had a cross word.' Moulton also added that Woodley, Towers and himself never actually met together.

Towers was equally appalled. At the time his only interest was in his

Source: Cartoon by Newman from *Sunday Times*, 16 April 2000. © Times Newspapers Limited

capacity as a member of the Training and Enterprise Council (TEC). When the TEC members heard the news of the Alchemy deal they knew that in effect it meant 'there would be no more business at Longbridge'. Naturally, Towers had an emotional attachment to the Rover group but he did not think anything could be done at that stage. Nevertheless, he spent the weekend 'making a few phone-calls, checking a few facts'. Eventually he put together a paper which he faxed to Richard Burden, the local MP for the constituency in which Longbridge was located. The paper suggested that 'maybe, just maybe, there was a possibility of an alternative to the Alchemy solution'. Towers said that the Phoenix name was a consequence of that first fax. 'I titled the fax, "Project Phoenix". I thought I can't call it "Project Rescue Rover". I even said on the fax, "apologies Richard for the unimaginative project name".'

Back at the DTI, suddenly Byers was no longer backing Moulton. Instead, he was encouraging the Nick Stephenson caucus to put a bid together. The Phoenix ambitions were further fuelled by a group of

20 Rover dealers, led by John Edwards, a well-known, Stratford-on-Avon based dealer, who started to compile a fighting fund to finance a counter-offer. The DTI then went further. It established a secret task force to co-ordinate a rival bid and foil Alchemy. As head of the task force, the department appointed John Towers. Towers met the 20 dealers. They wanted to promote a management buyout of the whole Rover operation, including Cowley and Mini. They were also threatening to sue BMW, because of the substantial investment they had been encouraged to make in their franchises to support the growth of the Rover brand. One idea was to use the threat of legal action to prise Mini out of BMW.

Towers then put Nick Stephenson in touch with the dealers, but Stephenson was cautious. He knew the deal they were attempting – which from the outset was predicated on keeping some form of volume production going at Longbridge – was going to be very difficult to make work. 'But we thought it might just be possible,' said Towers. The Rover brand was dead, Stephenson believed – although, unlike Moulton, he attributed its demise to BMW's mismanagement. If Rover was finished, then the 25, 45 and even the 75 could not work, because they were Rover badged. Another mass-market brand was needed.

By now, Towers was calling to find out what Stephenson and his colleagues had decided. The answer that came back was that they wanted the MG, Mini and, they thought, Triumph or Austin Healey – both of which retained a certain cachet as sporty saloons. They also wanted BMW to provide confidential information for a seven-day period, during which they would finalize their offer. And they wanted the DTI to use its good offices to ascertain which large-scale carmaker would supply a platform for the new mid-range model, the replacement for 25 and 45, that they knew they would need. Feelers were put out to DaimlerChrysler, VW – and Honda. Additional engineering support would be provided by Mayflower and Lola.

Towers arranged a meeting with Milberg and Samann at which he delivered the Phoenix demands. Behind the scenes, Byers was urging BMW to open the books to the consortium. But on Thursday 6 April Samann met Towers with BMW's response. The answer was, to put it mildly, discouraging. BMW would not let Mini go under any circum-stances. Nor would it sell any other British brands. And it was contractually obliged to honour the six-week exclusivity agreement with Alchemy. Phoenix could go ahead, but it was on its own.

That night, Towers, the dealers and Lola and Mayflower representatives held a council of war. They resolved to press on with their bid attempt, but they knew their prospects looked bleak. It was also decided, around this time, that Towers would move over from the DTI task force to head up the Phoenix bid. The biggest blow to the group was its inability to access the data that Alchemy had, because that trapped Phoenix in a Catch-22: without access to the information, it could not put together a proposal to win bank funding, and without bank funding it could not persuade BMW to take the offer seriously.

Nonetheless, the Phoenix members continued to bang on BMW's door. On 10 April, Towers and Stephenson met Luderitz to explain the details of their bid and how the finance was progressing. Towers has said that what happened was, in effect, a reversal of normal practice. Phoenix actually presented BMW with a business plan. Luderitz may have been unconvinced but he was certainly impressed with the level of detail in Phoenix's plan. Nevertheless he continued to tell Towers that his finances were uncertain and that he must substantiate the detail of the bid.

Like an action replay of Day and Simpson's attempts to launch a management buyout in 1993, Phoenix tried the big high street banks, including Lloyds and Royal Bank of Scotland, which had recently bought NatWest. All of them turned Phoenix down. The only exception was Abbey National, which started talks with the consortium and the dealers about providing at least £200m in commercial finance through its First National Motor Finance arm. What Phoenix needed, however, was to show BMW that it had the security of a bank facility, estimated at about £200m, to provide working capital. And that was what it did not have.

Alchemy's exclusivity period was due to end on Friday 28 April. By early that week, the Phoenix group had conceded defeat. Instead of going for Rover cars, some of the prime movers were preparing to switch their target to the powertrain operations and the Swindon pressings plant. Mayflower had been in on-off discussions with BMW for months about taking over Swindon, while Lola was interested in the engine and transmission business. Those businesses were of no interest to the Rover dealers. The consortium bid headed by Towers was on the point of dissolution.

Outside the ring fence surrounding Alchemy, Rover and BMW, public opinion in the West Midlands was running high against the deal. Already, Birmingham city centre had been the scene of marches against Alchemy, and there had been numerous calls to boycott BMW showrooms. The 'save our cars' mood had even percolated as far as west London. Near the flyover at the end of the M4 motorway, a construction firm erected a sign: 'Good Luck, Rover', it said. Consumers might have been unwilling to pay the prices and buy the cars that BMW needed to revive Rover, but the fate of the firm still bulked large in the national consciousness.

The fate of the firm still bulked large in the national consciousness

Moulton, true to form, was unconcerned about the popular discontent: 'At the end of the day, despite the enormous political and union noise, it had no bearing on our deal,' he said. He had also found someone to head MG: Chris Woodwark, a former Land Rover boss and later chief executive of Rolls-Royce Motors under Vickers. Moulton was much more concerned about the problems thrown up by the due diligence process. He and Walters were also baffled by the fact that BMW had a bare handful of people working on the deal. Moulton said: 'These guys were selling two giant businesses. Your average multinational gets heavyweight investment banking advice, but all BMW had, apart from its own people, were three fellows at Norton Rose doing both disposals. One of them practically had a heart attack in one of our meetings. We are used to dealing with chaos,' he said. 'What Ford made of it, God knows.' This poor soul was Hubert Grebenc who had been delegated responsibility for both disposals under the direction of Luderitz.

That was BMW's style: the Rover purchase had been handled identically, with Luderitz and a small Norton Rose team doing almost all the negotiations. Now, six years on, Luderitz was organizing the disposal that would unravel the strategy he and Pischetsrieder had devised. Inside BMW, the strategy chief was regarded as a man apart: 'Luderitz is a computer,' said one BMW executive. But he also felt deeply and strongly that a rational strategy had been destroyed by the British government's failure to keep the pound within limits, and he possessed an eccentric sense of humour, which also had a bearing on what followed.

On Thursday 27 April, Moulton, Walters and Bridges met the Norton Rose team at Camomile Street. The Alchemy side told them that there were 11 unresolved points that had to be settled before a final agreement could be signed – the eleven points constituted an agreed open items list. One big issue was what happened to the proceeds from the sale of Rover's thousands of stockpiled cars that BMW had made at cut-price levels since the letter of intent was signed. 'Our deal would only work if those hundreds of millions of pounds were put back,' Moulton said later.

Another issue, Alchemy said later, was a BMW requirement that Alchemy carry all the costs incurred by Rover until the deal was closed. Since the unions were threatening to lodge claims against BMW for having failed to consult on the Longbridge sale, Alchemy reckoned this item added £100m to its bill. Also, Alchemy said, BMW was only prepared to fund the state minimum severance pay for the 4000-plus workers that would leave Rover under the MG plan. Alchemy believed that, to avoid strike action, they would have to pay the enhanced terms contained in the original Rover agreement. That was another £100m on the costs.

BMW took a different view. It believed Alchemy had raised its cash demands from the £500m originally agreed to £700m. Later, the draft of Milberg's speech to the 16 May shareholders' meeting contained the assertion that Alchemy had asked for double the sum it had originally sought. However, Milberg did not make this accusation in the speech he actually delivered, and a furious Moulton resorted to his lawyers to obtain a retraction of the written statement. None of these issues was an inevitable deal breaker, and the two sides continued to negotiate. Then something happened. Moulton said: 'We went round the unresolved matters and about midday, they tabled a new issue.'

According to Moulton and Walters, BMW wanted Alchemy to guarantee £1bn of loans to the Rover dealer network worldwide, which BMW's finance arm had on its books. 'That had never been in the deal, and would have required us to take a view on the solvency of all the dealers, wherever they were,' Moulton said. 'We told them that we had no interest in doing this.' BMW had been spooked by the threat of legal action from dealers – the Germans as well as the British had been talking of lodging claims for compensation – but more importantly they had been taken aback by the strength of union, government and public resistance to the Alchemy bid. Alchemy, portrayed by the Phoenix supporters as the evil asset-strippers, had become a bête noire that the publicity sensitive BMW board could not ignore. Whatever the reason, the new BMW condition was totally unacceptable to Alchemy. Discussions continued at Norton Rose for the rest of the afternoon. Then, at 5.10 pm, Moulton and Walters started a conference call to Luderitz in Munich.

The conversation lasted half an hour, with the Alchemy duo trying to persuade Luderitz to drop the demand for the £1bn guarantee. Alchemy's funding structure could not support such a burden, they said. But BMW was insistent: the guarantee had to be given. That was it. There could be no deal. Moulton and Walters said goodbye to Luderitz and put down the phone. Then, with their lawyers from Macfarlane's, they went off to the Pitcher & Piano bar near Trafalgar Square. Instead of a celebration, it was a wake.

Inside Rover, news of the breakdown travelled fast. Less than an hour later, members of the 100-strong army of Alchemy accountants and advisers hunched over desks inside Gaydon and Longbridge suddenly found Rover security personnel at their shoulders. They were asked to surrender their site access cards, and quietly but firmly escorted off the premises. At 9 am the following day, Alchemy issued a media release that conformed to the unwritten City law which states: the importance of an announcement is in inverse proportion to its length. The one-line statement read: 'Alchemy Partners and BMW have ceased negotiations as they were unable to agree certain contractual matters, some of which arose yesterday.'

BMW's reaction was slightly less succinct, but not much: 'BMW Group will now pursue alternative routes to bring to an end its involvement in Rover car operations,' it said. 'Those routes include the sale of Rover car operations or its closure. A decision [on] which of these alternatives will be implemented will be taken during the course of next month.' Moulton and Walters's first thought was that BMW had decided it would be cheaper to close Rover than sell it on terms acceptable to Alchemy. Later they had a second thought: that BMW had decided there was a cheaper option than Alchemy which would still avoid the bloody business of closure: Phoenix.

Moulton believed a key factor was the legal advice BMW had obtained over its liabilities under the Insolvency Act. The Act contained a provision, known as the Transfer of Undertakings, that said any business which failed within two years of its disposal was assumed to have been insolvent at the date of the transaction. In those circumstances, the sale had to be unpicked and responsibility lay with the previous owner. 'As long as BMW believed it had that risk under the Insolvency Act, they had to sell to the people who would consume the least cash and had the least risk of going bust,' Moulton said. 'That was us, because of our smaller business model.'

However, Moulton believed BMW resolved that issue through an internal transaction that involved the sale of Land Rover – technically owned by Rover Group – to BMW at a very high price. That enabled BMW to discharge Rover's huge internal debts to its parent, and cleared the Insolvency Act hurdle. 'Once they got the clearance on the insolvency, they went for the buyer who wanted the lowest amount of money. We weren't far off £1bn different from the Towers alternative,' Moulton said.

Whatever the case – whether Moulton was right, or whether BMW simply concluded that the threats of legal action by unions and dealers would scupper its overriding objective of a quick, clean, no-strings exit – Phoenix now had its chance. But it did not have much time. BMW's reference to a final decision during May did not tell the whole story. In fact, Milberg and co. knew they had to bring the Rover issue to a conclusion by 16 May, the date of the next supervisory board meeting and the all-important shareholders' meeting. Indeed, the timetable was even tighter than that: for whatever Phoenix proposed to be properly evaluated, the consortium had to have its detailed plan in BMW's hands by the previous Friday 12 May.

But BMW, ever-sensitive to its image in Britain which could be seriously dented by a Rover shutdown, was keen to deal with Phoenix if at all possible. That much became clear when Samann issued an unlikely rallying call: 'It will be necessary to count on the support already promised in order to reach a quick and sound solution,' he said – referring to the pro-Phoenix noises made by Byers, the unions and the dealers. 'All parties – the state, the employees, the trade unions, the suppliers and our dealers will have to contribute their share.'

Phoenix went into action immediately. On Sunday, its advisers – led by Maghsoud Einollahi, a partner in Deloitte & Touche's Manchester office, and Jonathan Bartlett, corporate finance chief at the Birmingham-based broker Albert E. Sharp (which was owned by the South African group Old Mutual) arrived at Norton Rose's offices. Monday was the May Day bank holiday so face-to-face talks between Towers and Stephenson on one side and BMW's team on the other got underway on Tuesday. The start of the meeting was inauspicious: Norton Rose told Towers that it was already working on a different project called Phoenix, so they would have to codename this one Project Crufts. After all the bad media jokes about Rover being a dog, this was too much for the Phoenix team. They also felt the name reflected BMW's view of the buyout's prospects. They were partially reassured when the lawyers told them it was a standard name used by Norton Rose. What they did not say was that it was actually Alchemy's code name originally.

BMW then made the same offer to Phoenix that it had extended to Alchemy: it included £500m to take Rover cars away. But BMW made clear it remained concerned about how Phoenix was to finance a continuing operation on the scale it envisaged. Initially, Towers had talked about making 250,000–275,000 cars a year, but, after discussions with other members of the consortium, that figure was reined back to a more modest, but still audacious, 200,000 a year. No more than 2000 of the 8800 jobs at Longbridge were to be cut. At the DTI, Byers immediately threw his weight behind Phoenix: 'Whilst recognising that ultimately the final decision will be a commercial one to be taken by BMW, there is a role for government in bringing parties together and in leaving no stone unturned in trying to achieve a successful outcome for the workers at Longbridge,' he said.

Another Twist

But now came a further twist in the amazing Rover tale. While Byers had thrown himself behind the Phoenix bid, Number 10 Downing Street was taking a more sceptical view of its chances. The Cabinet Office had been tracking the course of the Alchemy negotiations. Indeed, Moulton and co.

found themselves being watched by three different Whitehall audiences: Number 10, Byers, and Byers's civil servants – some of whom were also concerned about the Phoenix plan.

Now, with Alchemy apparently out of the picture and Phoenix pushing its case, Geoffrey Norris, the Cabinet Office's industrial expert, became proactive. He canvassed City experts' views about Rover and the Phoenix plan. Then, late in April, he called a number of Britain's car industry leaders past and present – from both the carmakers and the component industry – to a Downing Street summit on Rover and Phoenix.

The experts' verdict was unanimous: the Phoenix plan was unviable

The experts' verdict was unanimous: in the prevailing environment of falling car prices and a hyper-competitive, over-producing European car market, the Phoenix plan was unviable. Longbridge could not survive and neither could a company straddling the specialist and volume sectors, as Phoenix would be with its output targets. 'You are either a niche maker of 50,000 cars a year or a mass manufacturer producing 5m cars,' said one industrialist.

This response confirmed Downing Street's nightmare scenario: that if Phoenix got Rover, there was a worryingly high chance that Towers and co. could fetch up on the doorstep of Number 10 on the eve of the next general election with an ultimatum that would reawaken memories of old Labour's worst days: give us more money or Rover will fail. Given the political importance of the West Midlands, that scenario would leave Tony Blair over a barrel. As the days ticked away towards Phoenix's mid-May deadline, a series of stories appeared in newspapers usually well-informed about Number 10 policy – notably *The Sun* – writing off Phoenix and preparing people for the closure of Longbridge. Phoenix members had no doubt that this was the Downing Street propaganda machine, briefing against them.

Indeed, few papers apart from *The Sunday Times* gave Phoenix any sort of chance of securing a deal. Stories in that paper recording Phoenix's progress, most of them written by David Parsley, who had followed the Phoenix bid attempt from the outset, were ridiculed in high places. Even Byers got back on-message. Early on Tuesday 2 May, as the Phoenix members were holding their first meeting at Norton Rose, Byers was meeting Jon Moulton. The encounter, which seemed to have the blessing of Downing Street, marked the formative stage of an effort to bring Alchemy back into the picture should, as most people expected, the Phoenix bid fail. Moulton then contacted BMW, but was given a dusty response.

On Friday morning, 5 May, Towers, Stephenson and Woodley – who was backing Towers to the hilt – met Byers at his Victoria Street offices and made a laptop presentation of their offer. The trade and industry secretary's previous pro-Phoenix ardour had conspicuously cooled – presumably, Phoenix supporters reckoned, because of the bucket of cold water that had been poured over him by Downing Street. Woodley, too, had experienced the pressure that was being heaped on Phoenix by the Labour establishment. He had refused to abandon his vociferous espousal of the Phoenix cause, and had been threatened with the sack by the TGWU top brass.

The DTI meeting was inconclusive: Towers could not reveal a firm source of funding, although he said two foreign banks were prepared to back Phoenix. Byers, who knew the British clearing banks had rejected the proposal, withheld his support. After frenetic telephone action over the next few hours, focusing on the bid financing, Towers arranged another meeting with Byers and the DTI. It took place at 1.30 pm and Einollahi, who had been brought along by Towers, said several overseas banks were prepared to provide a facility to fund working capital.

Then Towers and Stephenson asked Einollahi to leave the room. They had learned of the government's renewed contact with Moulton and they were furious. They threatened to pull out unless the government backed Phoenix and froze further contact with Alchemy. Byers listened. The Phoenix team left. Moulton, like most people, remained confident the bid would fail: 'We are waiting for Fawlty Towers to collapse,' he joked. But Alchemy, like the British government and almost every commentator, had overlooked one thing: BMW's determination to make a clean exit from Rover without inflicting the pain of an instant closure.

Alex Stephenson's task force had already concluded that a shutdown of Longbridge would cost 19,000 jobs in the West Midlands, and the effect would be felt among component makers much further afield. BMW executives did not want the blame for such devastation to land on them. Another element may also have been at work: many BMW executives genuinely felt that the strength of sterling rather than any mismanagement of Rover had caused the takeover to fail. And they laid the responsibility for the muscle-bound pound at the government's door.

End Game

Now BMW could see the government was at the very least refusing to back Phoenix – and at most, talking its chances of success down and laying the ground for a BMW-enforced closure. The last game of all in BMW's association with Rover was being played: pass the parcel. BMW was determined that, whatever happened, it was not going to be left to carry the can for a situation where ultimate responsibility, it believed, should lie at the government's door. Phoenix was its only hope of achieving that objective.

On Sunday 7 May, the *Sunday Times* reported that Phoenix was in talks with First Union Bank of North Carolina about a facility to provide the critical £200m working capital without which the offer seemed bound to fail. First Union, which owned 80 per cent of a British asset-based finance company called Burdale Financial, was America's sixth-largest bank. More relevantly, it was also well known to BMW because of its proximity to the Spartanburg plant in South Carolina. The speculative conclusion was impossible to avoid: BMW was the matchmaker that had brought Phoenix and First Union together, although the facility only ever existed as a proposal.

First Union's emergence was a clear indicator of what was about to happen. At 10 o'clock on Monday night, after two long days of negotiation, John Towers shook hands on a deal with the BMW lawyers at Norton Rose. They celebrated with a glass of champagne apiece and a bacon butty. By 8.30 the next morning, after a long night's work, the agreement was finalized. For a nominal £10, Phoenix would get the Longbridge factory, about 7000 workers, most from Longbridge and some from Gaydon, together with the Rover 25, 45 and 75, MGF and old Mini.

BMW would pay a total £500m in instalments: £275m immediately and £225m within three years. The money went to Techtronic (2000), the purpose-created company that actually bought Rover. Techtronic (2000) – not to be confused with a completely different business, Techtronic plc – had four directors: Towers, Stephenson, John Edwards, the dealer, and his finance director, Peter Beale. A small part of the total went in fees: Deloitte is believed to have received £6m for its work on Phoenix, and Albert E. Sharp £1m.

BMW's £500m payment was technically a loan, repayable in the event that Rover was sold. Like Alchemy, Towers was widely expected to seek an exit within three years, and possibly much sooner. Phoenix also took over the stocks of unsold Rovers: the First Union facility was secured on the value of these cars. On the Tuesday lunchtime, Towers drove up to Longbridge. He arrived in the early afternoon to a hero's welcome. Five years after his ignominious departure, it must have been a glorious moment:

> " Honestly, I thought we had no chance. We had to put a bid together without seeing the Rover books and Moulton was in exclusivity with BMW. The one thing I thought may just help us was if Moulton pulled out. He did, but our chances did not improve much then. We had a very short time to carry out due diligence and we had to meet the BMW deadline or Rover was going to close. We had no chance but, somehow, we made it ".

Actually, there was no mystery. The marriage of BMW and Phoenix was perfect. One partner was desperate to sell and the other desperate to buy. Phoenix, therefore, eventually got by with a little help from its friend – BMW. Satisfaction in Munich at the deal was total. One executive commented sardonically: 'It is right that the English should look after the English Patient.'

The marriage of BMW and Phoenix was perfect

A disgusted Moulton, who had conceived the idea, made the running, done the spadework and then watched as Phoenix seized the prize, focused on much the same point: 'Phoenix didn't know what was inside Rover and they didn't care. They did the deal at such speed and with such lack of due diligence that they couldn't conceivably absorb the details that we discovered.' Both those statements, from their diametrically opposed perspectives, implied the same thing: taking over Rover cars was the easy bit. Making a success of the business on the basis of at least 200,000 cars a year, as Towers had stated, was another matter.

Rover urgently needed a big brother, a volume carmaker that could at least spread the costs of developing a replacement for the 25 and 45, and at most be the buyer that would give Rover's owner an exit route. Honda's rapid rebuttal of an approach from its former partner highlighted the fact that it was in most carmakers' interest for Rover to disappear, rather than stay in business. The continuing slump in new car prices, which was eroding the value of Rover stocks and the residual values of all vehicles, was a sharp reminder of the high-risk strategy Towers and co. were pursuing.

One possible partner was Korea's Hyundai, but it was almost immediately annexed by DaimlerChrysler. That left Malaysia's Proton, owner of Lotus, which was keen to establish a European base. Talks with Proton began within months of the Rover deal, which took effect on 9 May. Towers was recapitulating the Rover–Honda relationship, offering Proton 20 per cent of the company in return for engineering and platform support, with a view eventually to selling it the whole business. In September, Rover was renamed MG Rover. Promotion of the MG name, the quest for a partner who might eventually buy the company – there were increasing similarities with Alchemy's plans for the MG Car Company.

BMW was past caring, even though Phoenix fetched up on its doorstep in September with a plea for at least another £150m on top of the £500m already agreed. With the economies of scale argument dead and buried, Milberg was humming a different tune: 'The yardstick for success is not the number of items, but profit margins achieved,' he told the *Financial Times*. Shorn of Rover and Land Rover, BMW still had the best margins in the business apart from Porsche.

Despite – and in some cases because of – the Rover sale, Milberg had suffered a rough ride at the 16 May annual meeting. One investor accused BMW of 'arrogance and ignorance' in its handling of Rover. The longest attack, almost 10 minutes, came from Rudolph Eisemann, a Heidelberg shareholder, who berated Milberg: 'You said you cannot drive a car by looking in the rear-view mirror. But what did you do? You drove the car right into a wall! Bang! Billions have been wasted since 1994. Rover was scrap at the time, the plant was scrap, waiting for the bulldozers to come.'

As ever, the Quandts kept their own counsel, except to issue a statement pledging their continued support for the BMW management, conditional on its performance in executing the new strategy. Certainly, the shares looked much healthier: by September, BMW was worth much more than Volkswagen, which had been seen as a predator before the Rover sale. Milberg was also hinting at co-operation with other carmakers: such comments lent weight to the expectation of many German experts that BMW would seal an alliance with VW at some point in the forthcoming 18 months. Pischetsrieder was now at VW, wearing the hat of quality director but tipped to inherit Piech's crown as chairman. Earlier, after his appointment was announced, the man who bought Rover told one associate, with a smile in his voice: 'Maybe I can improve the relations between Volkswagen and BMW.'

Milberg's verdict on Rover was given in BMW's 1999 annual report, published in March 2000. The statement was written when BMW still thought it would be selling Rover to Alchemy, before the emergence of Phoenix. Apart from that small detail, Milberg's final judgement was short and sharp. 'The Rover brand,' he wrote, 'was not strong enough to perform the tasks intended for it.' A multitude of sins – sins of commission and omission – lie behind those 14 words.

17
Lessons?
What goes round ...

AS WALTER HASSELKUS RIGHTLY SURMISED, BMW's ownership of Rover has become a classic merger and acquisition case study. Not, of course, the kind of triumphant case for which Sir Walter hoped. Instead, it may go down as perhaps the most graphic instance in recent business history of M&A 'worst practice'. From the day the acquisition was completed, almost everything that could go wrong, or be got wrong, did, and was.

The strategy, in its theoretical form was sound enough. Buy an off-the-peg volume manufacturer and keep the branding separate in order that the stronger brand would not be diluted while the new organization concentrated on building the weaker brand. But the strategy was less robust in practice than in theory. For one thing, the Rover brand (as opposed to Land Rover) was damaged goods. For another, BMW never came to grips with the Herculean task of implementing the strategy that had driven the deal.

The deal substantiated one of the oldest M&A laws in the book: that if a good medium-sized company takes over a struggling medium-sized company, the good tends to be driven out by the bad. Ford almost pulled the plug on Jaguar, a company one-hundredth of its size. BMW was not much larger, in output terms, than Rover. Not only did the German executives have very limited experience of dealing with foreign operations, they had never made an overseas acquisition of any size. As Karl Ludvigsen, chairman of the industry analysts Ludvigsen Associates and former vice-president of Ford of Europe, said early on: 'Remember, BMW doubled in size overnight when it bought Rover. Shocks to the corporate culture don't come much more dramatic than that. They may find Rover a bit more of a management problem than they anticipated.'

He could not have been more correct. Rob Golding, then the motors analyst at SG Warburg made a complementary point which has also been proved correct. He pointed out, 'Central to BMW's past success has been the development within the company of a culture that recognizes brand as the principal issue. The new BMW might just be too large to make sure that message is spread properly.'

Both statements also conceal a deeper truth. Bernd Pischetsrieder succeeded von Kuhnheim with a vision of a BMW whose independence he would secure by purchasing a mass producer and, at a stroke, doubling group traditional volume. To attain his critical mass goal, he had to find an ailing giant waiting to be bought. There was only one such company – Rover.

From that moment on Pischetsrieder was caught up in what psychologists refer to as the 'Concorde fallacy'. The 'Concorde fallacy' is so called because the Anglo-French airplane was financed even after it became obvious that by any economic calculations it should have been scrapped. Those responsible for the project had invested so much into it that they were unable to withdraw. Psychologists refer to the phenomenon as 'prospect theory'. They suggest that 'people are more motivated by their losses than their gains, and this results in increasingly risky behaviour as the losses accumulate'. In the gambling fraternity it is called 'chasing your money' – the idea that the only way to recover losses is by seeking ever longer odds bets.

Pischetsrieder implicitly admitted the validity of the theory when he argued that 'to withdraw from Longbridge would have meant acknowledging a reversal of strategy. The reason companies fail is because they do not have the courage to continue with the right strategy in the face of problems'. He was, as the statement shows, emotionally locked in to a strategy that had emerged from a perceived need to expand in order to protect BMW's independence.

This helps to explain some apparent inconsistencies in the implementation of the strategy. Interestingly, in our discussions with him, Pischetsrieder was keen to make a clear distinction between strategy ('with which nobody argued') and the implementation of that strategy ('in terms of financial sustainability'). When pressed on the desirability of separating the two, he was adamant that it was not only possible but essential. These are the words of a man on a mission, someone who, for whatever reason, has settled on a strategy and consequently invested so heavily in it that he is incapable of cutting his losses. For Pischetsrieder it was an emotional quest.

Throughout our interviews with all the major players the significance of emotional factors was predominant. For BMW people, for example, there was what Pischetsrieder referred to as an 'emotional attachment' to the company. He spoke of 'my cars', 'my company'. He always wanted what was best for BMW, even if that meant accommodating Reitzle, for example. The same was true of Reitzle, who spoke of the 5 February board meeting as a 'life-changing event. I had been at BMW for 23 years and I loved the company'. However, as strong as the emotional attachment to BMW was, the 'emotional resistance', within BMW, towards Rover. Reitzle was the lightning rod for that faction within the company. As Pischetsrieder put it, 'The problem was that my colleague, Wolfgang Reitzle, always officially followed the strategy but personally, within the company, opposed it.' Candidly, he admitted that although 'rationally there was an understanding that the strategy was right, emotionally there was a mood of resistance in the company'. 'I admit,' he said, 'that the emotional part was not well enough controlled.'

Part of the emotional baggage was a certain arrogance that the BMW way was the only way. In the light of its amazing resurgence under the Quandts' ownership such a belief was perhaps understandable. However, combined with an unwillingness to challenge the strategic imperative, such arrogance ultimately proved fatal. Pischetsrieder's final lament points the way to the real cause of BMW's Rover disaster. He said: 'We could have made Rover work if either the problems of the pound or the emotional problems had been absent – but having both damaged us.'

As Pischetsrieder suggests, Rover was not a monocausal collapse. There were many factors at play: The emotional aspects? Certainly. The pound? Definitely. They may have been the main ingredients but there was also more than a sprinkling of strategic blindness, a dose of factionalism including the personal rivalry with Reitzle, a history of mutual misunder-standing between the British government (both politicians and civil servants) and BMW – the two were never on the same wavelength – and a touch of cultural naiveté which generated managerial mistakes. The ultra-competitive environment and the particular pressure to cut car prices in Britain also played their part, as did the DaimlerChrysler merger. In the end, the number of factors conspiring to doom BMW's Rover strategy infused the whole story with the determinism of Greek tragedy.

All the forces at work combined to exert a level of pressure on the brand which it was ill equipped to resist. Milberg's 14-word epitaph said it all. If more thought had been given to the weakness of the Rover brand and less to the strength of the BMW brand, perhaps the brand too far would not have been attempted. As it was, the only way that BMW might have made the deal work was the one solution Pischetsrieder's strategy could not allow: blurring the lines between the two brands by producing BMWs in Britain. For Pischetsrieder, that was anathema. Yet it would have brought Rover, particularly Longbridge, the scale economies it needed to cover its losses during the highly vulnerable period when BMW was replacing the model range and rebuilding the Rover brand.

Two players emerged from the brand game with their reputations damaged and two with them considerably enhanced. The damaged duo were Pischetsrieder and Byers. Both badly misread signs and historical evidence although Pischetsrieder – 'a class act', in the words of one British investment banker who dealt with him – gained significant compensation with his high-level appointment at Volkswagen. The enhanced couple were Reitzle and Woodley. Both read the signs extremely accurately. Although Reitzle could be said to have overplayed his hand to the extent that he was ousted from BMW, he still managed to get, in the shape of Ford's premier auto division, his chateau in Bordeaux. Woodley consistently made accurate and insightful analyses of the situation which made his vehement opposition to Moulton so difficult to understand. Although superficially the Phoenix bid represented a better deal for Woodley's members, there was virtual unanimity among industry experts that the Alchemy solution offered a more realistic chance of Rover's long-term survival.

Where From Here?

Rover

In early September 2000 Jon Moulton predicted that Rover would be 'fighting for survival' by March 2001. Towers, who explained that he sees himself as involved in the 'stewardship' of the rechristened MG Rover, is determined to prove his old adversary wrong. When asked to give odds against Rover being in profit within a reasonable time frame he made two interesting comments. First he said, 'I don't actually care much about profit. All I care about is cash flow.' Second, he said, 'It's a racing certainty that we will succeed, we will be back in modest profit, probably with collaboration, in a couple of years' time.' The concentration on cash flow and collaboration both point to a preoccupation with an exit strategy. The protracted talks with Malaysia's Proton, the last independent carmaker of any size in the world that would be interested in a deal with Rover, offered Towers a route out of the business he had acquired amidst such drama. But the company he sells on, if he can sell it on, will bear little relation to the Rover that once existed. That Rover, the repository of the inheritance from Austin Rover, BL, British Leyland and the rest, reached the end of the road and effectively ceased to exist when BMW bailed out.

Despite the BMW cash sloshing around Rover, Towers' attempted rescue was always on dangerous ground. If he failed to find a big brother prepared to take over the business, his 200,000 cars a year strategy could leave Rover caught in no-man's land once more, between the volume production to which he had committed and the niche operation envisaged by Alchemy.

The source of the danger was the MG marque. If the new company simply slapped an MG badge onto products that were little more then re-branded Rovers – as BL executives had done in the 1980s with the MG Maestro and its ilk – then what equity the marque retained would soon be wasted. Towers would then find his last resort – reversion to the Alchemy MG strategy – cut off because the devalued MG name would no longer be able to support a credible business. Phoenix would end up saving fewer jobs even than Alchemy, because there would be nothing left worth saving.

Even if that nightmare scenario comes to pass, however, some good for British industry will still have come out of BMW's Rover takeover. Not for the car industry, but for the aerospace industry. By buying Rover, BMW saved British Aerospace. Had BAe been forced to limp on with the millstone to Rover's financing demands around its neck, it would have been a laggard in the subsequent consolidation of the western world's aerospace and defence industries. Its destiny would have been decided by others, in America or mainland Europe. Instead, liberated from Rover, BAe was able to seize a leading role in the restructuring – ensuring that the UK aerospace industry did not suffer the same fate as its much-diminished motor industry.

In this, as in so many respects of the BMW-Rover saga, history repeated itself. When Professor Sir Roland Smith bought Rover for BAe from the government in 1988, the injection of Rover into BAe's undercapitalised balance sheet saved the aerospace group from looming financial disaster. BAe was being severely exposed by huge exchange rate losses on sales of Airbus aircraft; without the reinforcement of Rover's large asset base, Smith knew that the company could have been forced into severe difficulty.

One purchase, one sale – but the same result. Rover had its uses, even if making cars was not one of them. The sad truth is that so much ground had been lost, and so much goodwill forfeited in the 20 disastrous years following the 1968 creation of British Leyland that even by 1988 there was no way back for Rover as a significant player under its own steam.

The only chance, as Margaret Thatcher realised when she tried to engineer the Ford takeover of BL in 1985/86, was to unite the company with a big player. The last real opportunity came in 1988 when Volkswagen was interested but was rebuffed by Lord Young. Rover could have become Skoda; the Czech car-maker; which VW eventually bought and has turned into a respectable business. It might not seem like much, but it would have been much more than is likely to survive.

BMW

BMW got out of its Rover jail almost free. Its share price surged in the aftermath of the Rover sale, as the profits on the continuing business reminded everyone that, next to Porsche, BMW still had the best margins in the industry. The euro's weakness against the dollar and the pound, the currencies of its two largest export markets, was fantastic news for the BMW brand. Profits and sales **BMW's future** in the year 2000 were heading towards all-time **is equally** records. Yet the laws of the twenty-first century **unpredictable** motor industry that drove BMW to the Rover acquisition still apply: over time, competition is likely to get tougher and it will become harder for BMW to recoup the increasing costs of keeping the marque at the leading-edge of the sporty, dynamic segment.

On 20 February 2000, Joachim Milberg told *The Sunday Times* that in 10 years' time BMW 'will be as independent as we are today and sell more cars than in our record year of 1999'. Milberg may have been right but the eventual outcome will probably be more complicated than either simple independence or a takeover. BMW will continue to attract the attention of predators, and there will be persistent questions about whether the younger Quandt generation will wish to retain all its current shareholding. If the Quandts do decide to sell they are unlikely to do so before early 2002, when the capital gains tax rates in Germany are due to be slashed. However, the most likely BMW move seems an alliance, falling short of a full merger, with a larger car company. Despite the interest of Ford, General Motors and Toyota, the probable partner is Volkswagen. Bernd Pischetsrieder may yet find himself closely associated with his old company. Only this time, Rover will be out of sight, if not quite out of mind.

Index